COOMBE ABBEY

COOMBE ABBEY

A History through Ten Centuries

Derek Winterbottom

ALONDRA BOOKS

Published 2018
Reprinted 2021

Published by
Alondra Books
37 King Edward Bay, Isle of Man IM3 2JG

Printed and bound by
The Copy Shop
Douglas, Isle of Man

ISBN No. 978-0-9567540-4-2

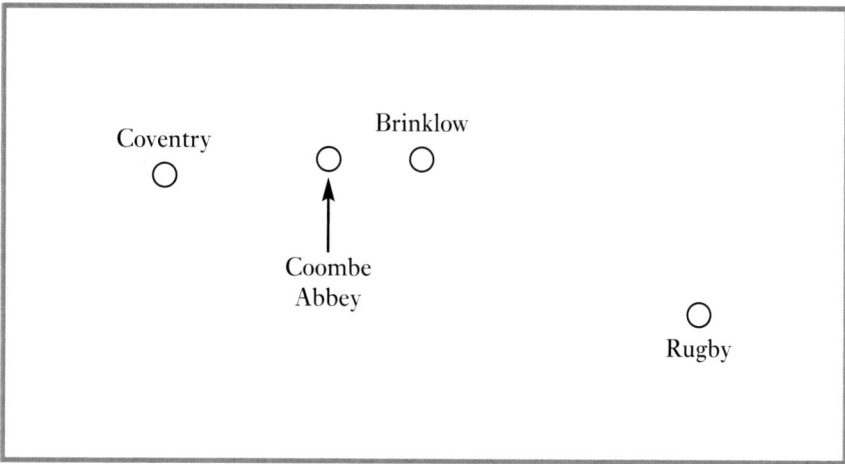

**Diagram of Coombe Abbey's location,
three miles east of Coventry**

CONTENTS

Chapter Five: The Victorians

Chapter Six: The American Heiress

Chapter Seven: Coombe after the Cravens

Appendix

PREFACE

I first visited Coombe Abbey Hotel in the summer of 2017 as a participant in the UK Open Backgammon Tournament and stayed there in a four-postered bedroom in the Cloisters for several days. I was fascinated by the house because it had clearly experienced a very long and also tortuous history which I felt it was time to re-tell. Robin Moore's paperback history of 1983 is no longer easily available, while another account by David Motkin, though very useful, is only accessible online. So I sat down to produce this book, writing in my winter base in the Canary Islands.

My first acknowledgement is to the work of the two authors already mentioned and I have also been lucky to receive valuable advice from Noel Chanan, the author of an authoritative study of the photographer second Earl of Craven, and Penelope Stokes, who provided me with a copy of her history of the village of Hamstead Marshall. I am also grateful for the help given by the staff of the Coventry City Archives and the British Library in London.

Coombe Abbey was officially spelt with only one 'o' until around 1900, so I have followed this convention. Further confusion may well be caused by the fact that for over three centuries most of the heads of the Craven family were called William, even when the heir to the family titles (as often happened) was a distant cousin.

Derek Winterbottom
Isle of Man
August 2018

Chapter One

The Monastery: 1150-1539

The Foundation

Nearly all the ancient records relevant to the medieval abbey at Combe, which was generally spelt with one 'o' until the twentieth century, have been lost or destroyed and the little that we do know is largely thanks to the work of the remarkable scholar and antiquarian Sir William Dugdale, who was born in Warwickshire in 1606 and educated at King Henry VIII's School in Coventry. He married and had nineteen children and bought the manor of Blyth, near his birthplace of Shustoke. As a result of a legal dispute with a neighbour he became fascinated by ancient documents and charters and began work on a history of Warwickshire: this took him to London where he established a friendship with the influential politician Sir Christopher Hatton, who became his patron. Dugdale was soon appointed one of the heralds at the College of Arms and became familiar with historic records held in the capital. When the Civil War began he supported Charles I and spent most of his time at the royalist capital, Oxford, working on the ancient manuscripts in the Bodleian Library. There he met Elias Ashmole, later the founder of the famous museum in Oxford named after him, who eventually married one of Dugdale's daughters. After the defeat of the king Dugdale made his peace with the Commonwealth and lived quietly at home at Blyth Hall working on a history of the English monasteries, which was followed in 1656 by his book 'Antiquities of Warwickshire', an exhaustive historical survey of almost every nook and cranny in the county. In 1677 Dugdale was knighted on his appointment as Garter Principal King of Arms and he died at Blyth in 1688. Much of the information that follows regarding the medieval abbey at Combe can be found in his astonishingly detailed history of Warwickshire which is based on early documents and charters.

The land on which Combe Abbey stands belonged before the Norman Conquest of 1066 to an Anglo-Saxon whose name was Harding but by the time of the 'Domesday' Survey in 1086 the king himself had taken possession of it – a fate which was typical of most of the property of the defeated Saxons. Described in the survey as the manor of 'Smitham' it contained the two villages of Over and Nether Smite (named after the Smite brook) and consisted of six 'hides' (about 720 acres) including woods a mile long and wide and it was valued in total at six pounds. William I distributed his conquered lands to 'tenants-in-chief' who held them in return for military service and they in turn passed them down to sub-tenants – a system much later called 'feudalism'. Either William I or his son Henry I gave the manor of 'Smite' to the formidable Norman warrior Robert de Beaumont, Count of Meulan and first Earl of Leicester, in return for one 'knight's fee', which was enough money to provide a fully armed and equipped knight for the lord's service. Either Leicester or his son handed the manor down to another Norman lord, Nigel d'Aubigny, who died in 1129. It was then inherited by his son Roger de Mowbray, who took the surname of his mother's family. He was aged only nine so he became a ward of the king (Henry I), who was responsible for his person and his lands until he reached the age of twenty-one.

Roger Mowbray was still a ward of Henry's successor, King Stephen, when he fought in 1138 at Northallerton where an invading Scottish army was defeated. After attaining his majority Roger remained a loyal supporter of Stephen in his contest with Matilda, the rival claimant to the throne, and he was captured, along with the king and many of his other supporters, at the battle of Lincoln in 1141. He was eventually released and then married Alice de Gant but left

England in 1147 to join the Second Crusade, led by Louis VII of France against Islamic forces in the Holy Land.[1]

Before he left for the Crusade, Roger de Mowbray granted his manor of Smite to Richard de Camville, a Warwickshire knight who was probably born in the vicinity around 1090 and who married Millicent, the widow of Robert Marmion. During his lifetime Marmion had been a notable benefactor of the Benedictines, granting land to the nuns of Polesworth Abbey in North Warwickshire and the monks of Bardney Abbey in Lincolnshire. But in the civil strife of Stephen's reign he attacked Coventry Castle, the stronghold of the king's enemy, Earl Ranulf of Chester, and expelled the nearby Benedictine monks of St Mary's Priory, using their buildings as a fortification. In the fighting which ensued when Ranulf came to the castle's rescue in 1144, Marmion was thrown from his horse into a ditch, broke a thigh and was captured by a common soldier who unceremoniously cut off his head.[2] After his marriage to Millicent Marmion, Richard de Camville, possibly under her influence, followed the example of her first husband and became a notable benefactor of the church and especially the newly-established order of Cistercian monks which had recently been introduced into England.

The monastic tradition in Europe mostly developed from the Rule of St Benedict who founded several monasteries in Italy in the first half of the sixth century, notably Monte Cassino. Religious houses for monks and nuns were gradually established throughout Europe and were strengthened in the tenth century by leadership provided by the abbots of Cluny, in Burgundy. But by the 1090s many monasteries had become too large and elaborate and their monks too worldly, paying insufficient respect to the original ideals of Benedict. In 1098 Robert, the Benedictine abbot of Molesme in Burgundy, moved with about twenty followers to Citeaux, or 'Cistercium' in Latin, a site south of Dijon, where he founded a new monastery whose monks would be committed to a reclusive life of hard work and constant prayer. Stephen

Harding, an Englishman, became the third abbot of Citeaux and drew up the 'Cara Caritatis' (Charter of Charity), essentially a constitution for the new order, which permitted the recruitment of 'lay brothers', who were not monks but farmed the land on which the monastery depended. In 1113 Bernard de Fontaine, a Burgundian nobleman aged 22, arrived at Citeaux at the head of about 30 of his friends and family and they were admitted to the order, which then entered upon a period of rapid and spectacular expansion, largely because of the administrative abilities of Stephen Harding and the outstandingly charismatic nature of Bernard's personality and leadership.

In 1114 Stephen Harding established a sister-house at Pontigny and in 1115 chose Bernard to create another sister-house near Langres, which he named Clairvaux. The regime that Bernard established there was very rigorous and disciplined but despite this it soon attracted some 130 enthusiastic new recruits, including his father and all his brothers. Another sister house of Citeaux was founded at Morimond in 1115 and three more at Mazan, L'Aumone and Loc-Dieu in 1120, 1121 and 1123.

The first Cistercian house in England was established in 1128 at Waverley, near Farnham in Surrey, by William Giffard, Bishop of Winchester, and the first abbot with some twelve monks came there from the abbey at L'Aumone. Waverley was very successful in establishing sister houses with the patronage of local lords, starting with Garendon, Leicestershire, in 1133 and followed by Forde, Dorset in 1136, Thame, Oxfordshire in 1137 and Bordesley, Worcestershire in 1138. There was then a pause before colonisation began again in 1147 with Biddesdon, Buckinghamshire and Bruern, all in Oxfordshire, and Merevale, the first of the Warwickshire houses, in 1148. This was founded by Robert de Ferrers, second Earl of Derby, but was relatively small and had only about ten monks, all drawn from Waverley. Ferrers requested that he be buried at Merevale, and fine contemporary stone effigies of himself and his wife can be seen in the gatehouse chapel which still survives there.

The ruins of Waverley Abbey, near Farnham, Surrey, the first
Cistercian monastery in England, established in 1128. Many
other English abbeys were colonized from Waverley, including
Combe in 1150.

The abbey at Combe was also colonized from Waverley thanks to the patronage of Richard de Camville, who on 10 July 1150 granted to Gilbert, the abbot of Waverley, his manor of Smite to fund the construction and maintenance of a Cistercian abbey. The abbey was dedicated to the Blessed Virgin (i.e. St Mary) and according to Dugdale the name 'Combe' referred to its 'low and hollow situation, the word 'Cwmm' in the British [language] signifying 'vallis' or 'convallis', as doth also 'Cumbe' and Combe' in the Saxon.'[3] Camville's generous grant of the manor of Smite to the Cistercians was subsequently endorsed by his immediate liege lord, Roger de Mowbray, who went further and relieved the abbey of the requirement to pay the manor's 'knight's fee'. Mowbray also granted the new abbey extensive woodlands at Binley and Burchleigh and also permitted the monks to keep cattle and pigs on their land without charges.

Finally, Robert de Beaumont, the second Earl of Leicester and justiciar of England from 1155 to 1168, ratified all these gifts as tenant-in-chief of the manor of Smite. In return, no doubt mindful of the fact that as justiciar Leicester was the second most powerful man in England after the king, the monks of Combe accorded him the status of principal founder of the abbey, promising that they would 'perform for him and his heirs such duties, both in his life time and at his death, as for their chief founders [i.e. Mowbray and Camville]'.[4] These duties were largely the regular praying by the monks for the souls of the departed founders, which was considered a great benefit on the soul's journey after death through purgatory and into heaven. Together with the need to expiate sins, especially the killing of other Christians, this explains why so many medieval magnates, from the king downwards, competed with each other to found religious institutions and make handsome donations to the church. Indeed in 1154 it was no less than Henry II, in the year that he succeeded Stephen as king of England, who effectively founded the third Cistercian abbey in Warwickshire at Stoneleigh, less than eight miles from Combe, by granting land in the forest of Arden to Cistercian monks who exchanged it for their property at Radmore, in Cannock Chase, Staffordshire, which they had found unsuitable.[5]

The abbey church

There was a Cistercian community at Combe for almost four hundred years, yet the information we have about it during those years is extremely limited, largely because it was forcibly closed down by Henry VIII in 1539 and the abbey church, together with nearly all its outbuildings, was later demolished. Fortunately, a cartulary, a register of about 300 charters relevant to the abbey, has been preserved in the British Library and it provides interesting, though often disjointed, details while other scraps of information surface at various times from which it is possible to construct an outline of the community's progress.

It seems that the first thing the monks did at Combe was to clear away the two existing villages of Over and Nether Smite (though not the parish church of St Peter) a move which Professor Maurice Beresford disapprovingly noted as being 'the county's oldest depopulations'. The monks of Stoneleigh were equally guilty and as soon as they arrived in Warwickshire, they 'removed the inhabitants from where they hoped to settle'.[6] This was because Cistercian monks worked on their land, which they either tilled for crops or used as pasture for animals, especially sheep. The famous Cistercian abbeys of Fountains and Rievaulx, both founded in Yorkshire in 1132, developed over time into sheep farmers on a vast scale, bringing them great wealth through the sale of wool – the oil of medieval England – but neither Combe nor Stoneleigh could develop on this scale because they did not own such large tracts of land.

Apart from the manor of Smite itself and the woods at Binley and Burchleigh granted by Roger de Mowbray, the monks of Combe gradually acquired other lands through grants and bequests from pious individuals. Dugdale provides an exhaustive list of these which it would be tedious to reproduce in full but Roger de Mowbray's son, Nigel, gave the rest of the woods at Binley and Burchleigh, a grant later confirmed by his son, also Nigel. In general, the parcels of land received by the abbey were small, but there were a good many of them. The priory of St Mary at Coventry gave 60 acres of land in Binley, Thomas de Stoke gave 24 acres in Withybrook and all his arable land in Binley. Agatha le Strange gave land in Wolston and Walter Spigurwell pasture land at Blakedon. John de Chalvini gave his manor of Little Lawford. Reginald Basset gave part ownership of the church at Wolvey, while Thomas Trove gave lands in his manor of Shirford. John de Merston gave property in Merston, Binley and Coventry which he willed should be used to provide shoes for the poor at the gate of Combe abbey. Many houses in Coventry were given to the abbey by individual citizens, and in Staffordshire the monks received an impressive 240 acres at Trescote from William, the son of Wydon. In the middle years of the thirteenth century the monks bought the manor of Little Copston while the manor of Brinklow itself was granted to them in 1345 by William Thorpe.[7]

In addition to gifts of land and property, the monks also received various valuable immunities and tax exemptions. As early as 1156 Henry II granted the monks 'free warren', or the right to hunt small deer, hare, rabbits, etc. on their land. He also granted them important judicial powers, namely the right to question and judge any suspected criminals apprehended on their land, as well as immunity from services to the county or hundred court, and most important of all, immunity from paying tolls and customs normally due to the crown. In the early years of the abbey, a row broke out between the monks and the canons of Kenilworth to whom Roger de Mowbray had granted the tithes (a church tax of ten percent) from the parish of Smite before the monks arrived in 1150. The canons then found this revenue reduced because, thanks to papal dispensations, Cistercian monks generally claimed immunity from tithes on land they tilled. The canons appealed to Archbishop Thomas Becket who directed that the abbey should pay the canons the same amount of tithes as they had received before 1150. The monks were not at all happy with this and appealed to Pope Urban III who appointed a later archbishop, Baldwin, to review the matter. He managed to achieve a compromise in 1187 by which the monks were excused payment of some tithes but undertook other responsibilities, such as providing divine service in the parish church at Smite.[8]

The most important task that faced the first monks at Combe, once they were assured of a suitable site, together with adequate funding, was the construction of an abbey church, cloistered cells, a kitchen, lavatories and other amenities. They were led by their first abbot, named Martin, who was in charge of the community for 27 years and may well have been responsible for most of the permanent buildings. They were constructed with the reddish sandstone local to the area which had already been used around 1100 at St Mary's priory in Coventry and which was being used at the parish church of All Saints at about the same time that work began at Combe. It may be that craftsmen and master builders from Coventry were employed for the architectural planning, with the monks and lay brothers doing some of the manual work.

Very little trace remains today of the abbey church at Combe, but its nave stood where the moat and bridge are at the entrance of the hotel today and the original cloisters lay on the footprint of the present three-sided quadrangle. According to the architectural historian Geoffrey Tyack, the late 12th century buildings of the abbey

> ....were arranged around a cloister to the north of the church, with the chapter house in the east range, approached through a round-arched doorway of red

sandstone, the refectory to the north, and a range of buildings for the lay brothers in the west range....the 12th century entrance to the chapter house still survives, as do the 15th century windows to the north and west cloister walks.[9]

We do not know exactly what the abbey church looked like but it probably copied the simple 'Early English' style employed by the first Cistercian abbeys in Britain. There are still substantial ruins at Waverley and these provide a good guide to the form Combe Abbey might have taken. Moreover, there is still one original arch from the chapter house which is incorporated into the fabric of the present hotel's entrance lobby. Combe Abbey was never intended to be a huge church, such as were eventually built in magnificent style at Fountains and Rievaulx and at Tintern in Wales, but it was no doubt handsome enough. According to a sketch plan drawn by Victorian architects who uncovered the foundations of the abbey church, the aisled nave had nine bays and the piers were circular with square bases. The four or five-bay presbytery was also aisled and the overall length of the church was 250 feet (76m) or possibly more. The transepts were of 'squat proportions' with two chapels in each and the dimensions of the cloister were 111.6 feet square.[10]

The aim of the new Cistercian communities was to adhere as closely as possible to the original Rule of St Benedict and to live a life devoted to prayer and manual labour, preferably in a location as remote as possible from the wider world. Dugdale, writing in the seventeenth century when there were still hundreds of Cistercian communities on the continent, emphasised the austerity of their life. The monks did not leave their cloisters unless to go to prayer or work, nor did they generally speak to anyone except the abbot or the prior (his deputy). Their dress was a coarse woollen habit, coloured white as opposed to the Benedictine black and they prayed and sang the prescribed services

Top: an ingenious modern model of the abbey of Merevale, Warwickshire, founded in 1148. The almost contemporary abbey at Combe (1150) might have looked very similar, except that, possibly for topographical reasons, the abbey church at Combe had its cloisters on the north side rather than the south. (see diagram below).

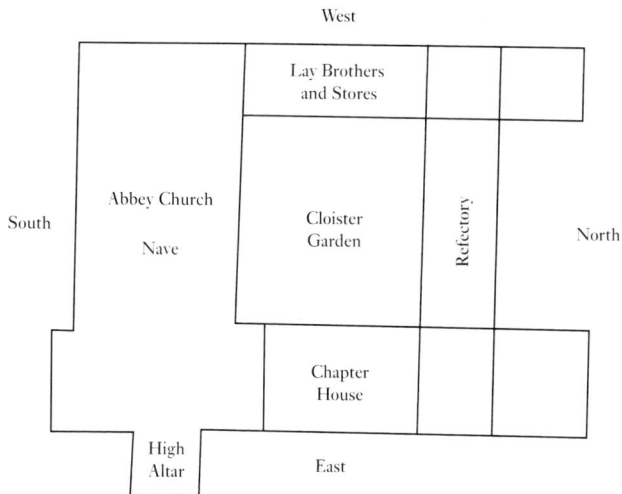

West

	Lay Brothers and Stores		
Abbey Church Nave	Cloister Garden	Refectory	North
	Chapter House		

South

High Altar

East

most of the day and much of the night. Food was simple, and 'the abbot assumes no more liberty to himself than any of his [brothers], everywhere being present with them and taking care of his flock .... wheresoever he eats he is abstemious of talk, or any dainty fare...' It was the duty of the monks to take care of strangers, sick people and any who came to the abbey for help, while they themselves 'do devise extraordinary afflictions for their own bodies, to the intent their souls may be advantaged'.[11]

The monks as sheep-farmers

Although the monks of Combe never developed into sheep farmers on a huge scale because they lacked the acreage, they made the best of what they had and developed 'granges' or farms on their land, which provided pasture for many hundreds of sheep. Their wool would then perhaps be sent to nearby Coventry from where it would in the early years have been sent across to Flanders to be made into high-quality cloth and later on be used to make cloth in Coventry itself. Records found in Coventry suggest that cloth-making was already the predominant industry during the twelfth and thirteenth centuries and by 1377 the city was so prosperous as to be considered the fourth richest town in England, after London, York and Bristol, the famous spires of its three largest churches soaring into the sky to emphasise the town's importance. But sheep-rearing was big business and it inevitably involved Cistercian monks throughout the country in financial dealing that in theory should have been beyond the remit of their Order. The taxation records of 1291 show that the abbey's revenues from their six farms amounted (to the nearest pound) to nearly £66 a year, while other properties brought in almost £70 a year, making Combe, 'at that date, by far the wealthiest [monastic] house in Warwickshire'.[12]

A depiction of a shepherd, his sheep, and a 'barkable dog',
from an illuminated Bible, c.1250.

Professor Eileen Power, in her splendid lectures on the medieval wool trade given in Oxford in 1940 at a time when enemy bombs were raining down on London and would soon destroy much of medieval Coventry, complained that cross-breeders since the eighteenth-century had so changed the appearance of sheep that they had 'defaced an irreplaceable collection of walking documents' and that what medieval sheep actually looked like we can only now guess.[13] There were probably two main types, one of which was a small sheep producing short wool which was used to make heavy cloth, the wool having been thickened by fulling, a smelly and unattractive process involving being trampled by human feet in stale urine. The other type was a larger sheep, producing longer wool which was combed and used for lighter cloth. According to Power, 'The great bulk of the fine wool exported in the middle ages came from two long-woolled breeds, Cotswolds and Lincolns, and, some way behind, Leicesters, which were probably common to most of the Midlands'.[14]

Given that sheep farming was the main occupation of the countryside, the shepherd was an important figure in medieval life, and a thirteenth century treatise on estate management gave this advice:

> It profiteth the lord to have discreet shepherds, watchful and kindly, so that the sheep be not tormented by their wrath but crop their pasture in peace and joyfulness; for it is a token of the shepherd's kindness if the sheep be not scattered abroad but browse around him in company. Let him provide himself with a good barkable dog and lie nightly with his sheep.[15]

The golden age of English wool production was between about 1200 and the 1320s and there was then a slowdown in growth to about 1400 and stagnation thereafter. The reasons for this were mostly political and included the disruption caused by warfare, competition from other European producers and punitive taxes on wool imposed by a crown which had to cope with constant inflation. The main way monasteries sold their wool was that a dealer would make a cash offer for the wool crop for one or possibly several years in advance but this deal could go badly wrong for the monastery if it misjudged future production.[16] The records of the Cistercian Pipewell Abbey in Northamptonshire show that it got into serious difficulties between 1314 and 1321, which was in any case a time of great hardship throughout northern Europe. There was exceptionally bad weather, with heavy rains and cold winters, and this ruined harvests and caused famine for the almost biblical span of seven years. So a monastery could not afford to mishandle its wool contracts. But at Pipewell it was recorded by a monk who had once been abbot that:

> By reason of seven years of sterility and murrain amongst the animals, the goods of the house of Pipewell were so completely used up that the residue thereof sufficed not for the slender sustenance of the monks, but sometimes they sat down in the refectory for three or four days with only black bread and pottage ....[17]

Debts, murder, plague and civil war

Combe Abbey also experienced serious problems in the first quarter of the fourteenth century and despite its wealth it managed to get itself seriously into debt, apparently because of 'defective rule' under an abbot called William, elected around 1283, and another called Richard, (1328-1332). In 1325 Edward II granted Abbot William the right to hold a market at Wolvey every Wednesday and a three-day fair annually on the feast of St Mark, presumably to help with the finances, but in

1332 Abbot Richard had to apply for royal protection because the abbey 'was burdened with debt and reduced to much distress'. The king appointed William de Clinton and Robert de Stretford to act on his behalf to sort out the problems and John de Pulteney, a citizen of London, helped out with £40 while John de Merynton, of Warwickshire, provided a very generous £140 to reduce the debts. Not surprisingly, Abbot Richard resigned that year.[18]

His successor, Abbot John, was clearly considered a more capable individual because he was appointed bishop of the Irish diocese of Cloyne in 1335 after a dispute between the Pope and King Edward III which was eventually settled along the lines that the Pope had the right of appointment but the new bishop had to take a vow of fealty to the king as a landowner. Abbot John's successor Geoffrey has become famous in the history of Combe because of the shocking fact that in 1345 he was apparently murdered in his own abbey. No-one knows why or by whom, despite the fact that the king immediately appointed six of his judges to conduct an inquiry into the outrage. Geoffrey was not Archbishop Becket, but for an abbot to be murdered on the hallowed ground of his own abbey was a crime of major importance. The jury was composed of men from Northamptonshire, to secure impartiality, but if they ever found out what happened, the records have been lost. Needless to say, in the days when Combe became a large mansion house the legend of the murdered abbot, wandering through the corridors in his white robes seeking revenge against his killers provided the perfect ghost story.

One disaster followed another because in 1348 the so-called 'Black Death' arrived in England from the continent, an unprecedented plague which claimed the lives of about a third of the population of England. Those who died included Geoffrey's successor as abbot and some of the monks.[19] A second plague struck in 1362 and two more up to 1379. One of the long-term effects of the plagues was a dramatic decline in the population and a reduction of the number of men available to work in the fields. This, in turn, led to a major change in the 'feudal system' because men were able to avoid being tied to work on their lord's land and moved away in search of wages. In the monastic houses the number of lay brothers declined because they could earn more elsewhere, so abbey lands were increasingly leased out, which turned the monks even more into 'capitalists'.

By 1300 there were about 500 Cistercian houses in Europe, and that number climbed to a peak of 750 in the fifteenth century. All Cistercian abbots were required to attend meetings of the General Chapter of the Order, usually held at Citeaux, and several documents have survived which granted the king's permission to various abbots of Combe to cross the Channel for this purpose. However, it is clear that between 1350 and 1530 many Cistercians, like the Benedictines before them, relaxed their determination to live a life of austerity and manual work and tended to concentrate on scholarship and prayer, leaving the running of their farms and estates to lay employees.

The wealth of Combe Abbey was increased in 1429 when the pious King Henry VI granted it rights over the parish church at Naseby in Northamptonshire, which included the appointment of the vicar and revenues from its glebe lands. But the middle of the fifteenth century was a period of considerable disruption in England because of a prolonged civil war (1455-1487) initially caused by the rebellion of the Duke of York, heir to the throne of his cousin, Henry VI, a feeble and inadequate ruler. Lawless acts became common and it was not unusual for monasteries to be attacked, partly because there was a rising mood of anti-clericalism throughout the nation and partly because many monasteries were considered in their localities to be harsh landlords, sometimes collecting rents illegally and even stealing livestock.[20]

It seems that Abbot Richard of Combe had this reputation and on 28 July 1451 Combe was attacked by Sir Thomas Malory of Newbold Revel at the head of about a hundred men. According to one

The ruins of two of the greatest Cistercian abbeys.
Top: Fountains, near Ripon in North Yorkshire and (bottom)
Tintern, in Monmouthshire, South Wales.

account 'they broke by night into Combe Abbey breaking down eighteen doors with huge baulks of timber and insulting the abbot and the monks. They broke open two of the abbot's chests, stealing £21 from one and £25 in gold and silver marks from the other. Next they went into the abbey church and took jewels and ornaments to the value of £40 and escaped into the night'.[21]

The remarkable thing about Malory is that he was a member of the upper class; a landowner, knight and member of parliament. Up to 1450 he had pursued a respectable and even distinguished career but as a Yorkist supporter he became caught up in the Lancaster-York conflict and he was accused in 1450 by the Lancastrians of ambushing one of their number, the Duke of Buckingham, probably because he was a supporter of one of Buckingham's rivals. Why he chose to attack Combe is not clear, but for this and other acts of lawlessness he was tried at Nuneaton in 1451 and committed to prison in London for a year. Over the next decade he was accused of many acts of lawlessness by his enemies and spent several spells in prison, often escaping. He was eventually pardoned in 1461 when the Yorkist King Edward IV came to the throne. Most scholars are of the opinion that during one or other of his spells in prison he wrote 'Le Mort d'Arthur', considered to be the first major work of English prose, telling the story of the Arthurian legend in twenty-one books with 507 chapters. Printed by William Caxton in 1485 it has subsequently become a world-famous classic text.[22] In 1470, one of the most turbulent years of the civil war, when Edward IV was struggling to retain his throne, he visited Combe Abbey, it is said, but whether Sir Thomas Malory was with him is not recorded. Faced with a serious rebellion Edward was forced to flee the country but returned in 1471 and defeated his enemies at the battles of Barnet and Tewkesbury, restoring a measure of peace for the next dozen years.

Combe Abbey survived all these upheavals and though unpopular in some circles the monks by the next century were found to be generous in their gifts to the poor, because 'four shillings and eight pence in money, ten quarters of rye bread at five shillings a quarter, three quarters of malt beer at four shillings a quarter and 300 herrings at one shilling and eight pence a hundred were distributed to the poor at the abbey gate'.[23] Moreover, the abbey continued to receive benefactions, such as that of Sir Richard Farnborough who in his will of June 1509 left £30 to build the south side of the cloister, and to put glass (an expensive luxury) in the windows. He also left one pound to the abbot, half a mark (six shillings and eight pence) to every priest and a quarter of a mark to every lay brother in return for the conducting of services each year to mark the anniversary of the deaths of his wife and himself.

The Dissolution

The monks were able to enjoy their new glazed cloister for only another thirty years before they were bundled out and their abbey shut down by the firm hand of the Tudor king, Henry VIII. He was determined to secure his upstart dynasty by enriching the crown, reducing the power of the great nobles and enlisting the support of the gentry classes by selling them land formerly owned by the church. There was nothing particularly new about Henry's resentment of the power and wealth of the Church of Rome, nor did his determination to destroy the monasteries derive only from his matrimonial problems. The potential for conflict between secular rulers and the heads of the Roman Catholic Church had always been great, especially from about 1200 onwards when popes increasingly attempted to assert universal authority over all Christian sovereigns. English kings, in particular, resented the authority of a pope far across the seas, unless it suited their purpose of the moment, and they quarrelled on a regular basis with the Pope over matters of appointments to bishoprics and other emoluments, especially when absentee foreigners (often Italians) were involved.

As early as 1351 Edward III's parliament passed a Statute of Provisors restricting the Pope's power of appointment in England, while another statute in 1353 ('Praemunire') made it illegal to appeal to the Pope in disputes over appointments. Hostility to the papacy was increased by the fact that from 1309 to 1376 seven successive popes were based in Avignon and all of them were French and under the influence of the king of France at a time when England and France were locked into the conflict known as 'The Hundred Years War'. Even worse, when one pope did return to Rome, the Avignon cardinals elected another one in Avignon, so that between 1378 and 1417 there were two competing popes, both denouncing each other.

Criticism of the Roman church was led in England by John Wycliffe (c1325-1384) who objected to the very idea of the papacy, the wealth and worldliness of church leaders (i.e.bishops and abbots), the insincerity of monks and friars, the ignorance of many clergy, clerical celibacy, papal taxes (annates), the selling of indulgences (pardons for offences) and even the crucial question of whether the bread really did become the body of Christ in the Mass. Wycliffe's followers were nicknamed 'Lollards' or 'mutterers' but they had many friends in high places, though they risked dire penalties for heresy. The Hundred Years War (1337-1453), followed by the Wars of the Roses (1455-1487) kept English kings diverted from the formidable task of reforming church institutions and they took a repressive line against heresy. When Henry Tudor established peace at the end of the century and the crown passed to his eighteen-year-old son Henry VIII in 1509, steps towards reform began to be taken, especially after the devastating attacks on corruption in the church made by the writings of the Dutch theologian Erasmus (1466-1536) and the German priest, Martin Luther (1483-1546), both contemptuous of popes who, during the Renaissance, had been notoriously corrupt and worldly.

In the early years of his reign Henry VIII allowed his exceptionally able and energetic minister Thomas Wolsey to govern his administration. Wolsey was a priest who rapidly rose through the ranks under the king's patronage and was appointed bishop of Lincoln and archbishop of York in 1514, and Lord Chancellor the next year when, at Henry's request, he was also created a cardinal by the Pope. This gave him precedence over the existing archbishop of Canterbury, increased when he was appointed papal legate in 1518. Despite many other calls on his time and energy, such as financing and administering a war against France and reforming the judicial and taxation system, Wolsey made a start on the reformation of monastic life in England, dissolving about thirty of the worst examples of decadent houses and in most cases putting the resources gained to good use by founding schools, or colleges at the universities, such as what became Christ Church at Oxford and Jesus College at Cambridge, both former priories.

Wolsey fell from power in 1529, largely because he was unable to secure an annulment of Henry VIII's marriage to his first wife, Katherine of Aragon. The king then turned to his minister Thomas Cromwell who managed to persuade Parliament to accept the doctrine that in England the king and not the pope was head of the church. This was enshrined in law by the Act of Supremacy in 1534 which, in addition to enabling the king to authorize his own divorce, effectively gave him unfettered power over the 800 or so religious houses and the land they owned, amounting to about a third of England. The first decision made was that all church land should pay a 10% tax to the crown, so in January 1535 Cromwell organized a valuation of the church ('Valor Ecclesiasticus'), sending commissioners out to demand from all owners of church property a statement of their income given on oath. Many of the commissioners were unpaid ecclesiastics, gentry and JPs: they worked hard and by the middle of the summer their task was complete. At the same time a separate group of commissioners

A portrait of Thomas Cromwell after Hans Holbein
the Younger. (NPG)

visited religious houses in order to report on any abuses, whether of a sexual nature or spiritual – such as superstitious reverence given to relics.

The 'Valor' was the first comprehensive survey of the church in England and the king and Cromwell were not slow to realize that they now had an unprecedented opportunity to increase the wealth of the crown by closing down monasteries and taking their lands. Hence in February 1536 an Act was passed authorising the closure of all religious houses with an annual revenue of less than £200. The preamble to the Act made it clear that 'manifest sin, vicious, carnal and abominable living is daily used and committed among the little and small abbeys, priories and other religious houses of monks, canons and nuns, where the congregation of such religious persons is under the number of twelve persons' and went on to declare that despite many attempts to reform and improve monastic life over many years, no progress had been made and the existing small monasteries were effectively dens of vice, committed to 'unthrifty, carnal and abominable living' where 'vicious living shamelessly increases and augments'. No doubt the commissioners had uncovered examples of homosexual practice (which is what the preamble meant but did not actually say) but a degree of exaggeration, if not gross exaggeration, by the law-makers must be assumed. The Act authorised the king to dissolve these monasteries, with their lands reverting to the crown.

According to the 'Valor', some 453 religious houses had an annual income of less than £200, but the king could make exceptions and in fact less than half this number were dissolved in the first wave of 1536.[24] Combe was not one of them because, in any case, it had just squeaked over the limit with a declared income of £211 and fifteen shillings. Most houses due for suppression accepted their fate, though the monks of Norton Priory in Cheshire and Hexham Abbey in Northumberland resisted and paid the penalty - imprisonment for the former and execution for the latter. At first there does seem to have been a genuine intention to reform institutions because monks from some suppressed houses were moved to larger monasteries and the king even set up new foundations – for example at Bisham Priory near Marlow which took in monks from the suppressed abbey of Chertsey and was refounded as Bisham Abbey.

Despite the fact that in the past there had been widespread criticism of monasticism and demands for reform, Henry VIII's decision to assume headship of the Church and close down so many religious houses came as a shock to many faithful Catholics, especially in the conservative North where what amounted to a rebellion broke out in Lincolnshire and Yorkshire in October 1536. Led by a lawyer, Robert Aske, it was backed by over thirty thousand people calling themselves 'The Pilgrimage of Grace'. The King deviously promised to halt the dissolutions and the rebellion dispersed, after which Henry had 216 of the ringleaders rounded up and executed for treason, including the Cistercian abbots of Jervaulx and Fountains as well as four other abbots, 38 monks and 16 parish priests.

The expected windfall for the royal coffers did not materialise from the dissolutions of 1536, largely because of administrative expenses and the need to pay pensions to the evicted abbots and monks. Throughout 1537 and 1538 Henry and Cromwell increasingly made it known that the voluntary surrender of the remaining houses by their abbots would be welcomed, and that generous pensions would be paid for life. As it was quite clear that refusal might be interpreted as treason and that the house might be dissolved anyway, the vast majority of abbots and priors were prepared to co-operate.

Cromwell was assisted in the process of dissolution by a number of agents, one of whom was Dr John London, born in 1486 and educated at Winchester College and New College, Oxford, where he became a fellow in 1505 and gained a doctorate in 1519. He was an ordained priest and held posts at York Minister and Lincoln Cathedral before his appointment as Warden of New College in 1526. In 1535 he became a commissioner for the visitation of monasteries and between then and 1538 he played an important part in the dissolution of houses in Oxfordshire, Warwickshire and Northamptonshire. Early in 1538 it seems that either he or another of Cromwell's men managed to persuade the existing Abbot of Combe, Oliver Adams, to retire in favour of Robert Kynner, who was thought to be more likely to co-operate in a surrender deal.

In September London reported this to Cromwell and in December he was in Coventry supervising the suppression of the Carthusian house there and reminding Cromwell that Combe was only a few miles away and that he would be pleased to 'go through' with it also because he felt that Cromwell 'could not have a more commodious house than Combe Abbey, and that the longer he waited in seizing it the worse it would be'. However, Abbot Kynner clearly had good negotiating skills because London reported back early in January 1539 that the abbot 'labours to have the house continue longer…it is hard trusting those whose coats and hoods be sewn together.' Towards the end of the month Kynner had been 'persuaded' to give in and on 21 January the abbey and all its lands and possessions was formally surrendered to the king by Abbot Kynner, the former Abbot Oliver and thirteen other monks. Kynner's 'sweetener' was a huge pension of £80 a year for life, with around £6 to each of the monks. The ex-abbot, however, got nothing.[25]

It is difficult not to see trickery, bribery and underhand deals in all of this, especially when we find that the Sheriff of Coventry subsequently informed London that Kynner had hidden £500 in a feather bed at his brother's house. The bed was searched, but only £25 was found – the ex-abbot explaining that he had spent it all defraying his debts.[26] Moreover, London himself was far from beyond moral reproach: he was accused of improper behaviour towards nuns while dissolving the nunneries at Chepstow and Godstow and he was obliged to do public penance for adultery in Oxford on another occasion. His

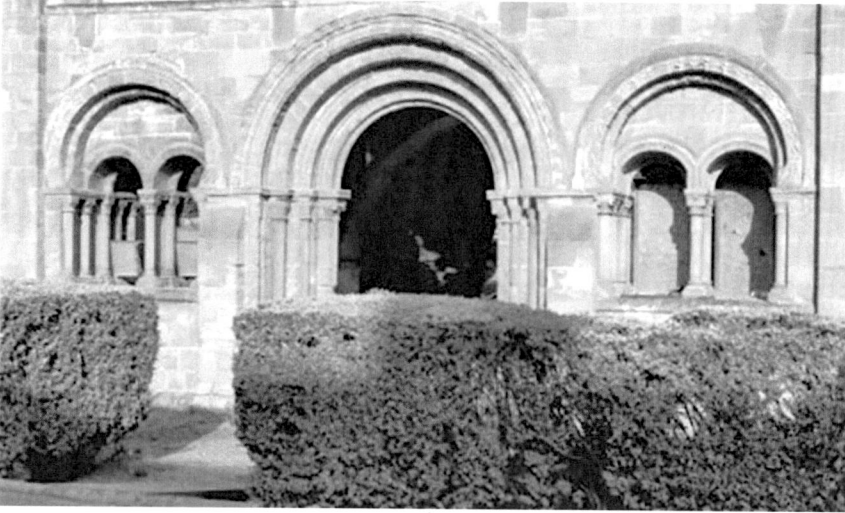

The only remaining features of the original Combe abbey
buildings (though somewhat restored) are this archway which
led to the former Chapter House, and the adjoining arched
windows. They can currently be seen as part of the present hotel
entrance lobby.

ultimate downfall came in 1543 when he and others brought charges
of heresy against Archbishop Cranmer for his increasingly 'Protestant'
views. The king supported Cranmer on this occasion and London was
condemned to ride backwards on a horse through Windsor, Reading
and Newbury, and to be placed in the pillory in each town. He lost his
ecclesiastical appointments, was imprisoned in the Fleet and died soon
afterwards that year. No doubt the many monks and nuns who had
been evicted by him were not particularly sorry.[27]

Chapter Two

From monastery to mansion, 1539-1620

The first secular owners, 1539-1581

About 800 religious houses were closed down between 1535 and 1540. Fourteen of the great monastic cathedrals survived, without their monks, while about a hundred other former monastic churches still survive today in whole or in part because they were bought by a benefactor or the local community and used as parish churches. Nearly all the rest had the valuable lead stripped from their roofs and guttering, leaving the churches to decay and become picturesque ruins, as many still are today. In some cases the church disappeared completely, usually because the stone was sold or used to build a domestic dwelling nearby. Although the crown did benefit substantially from the sale of the monasteries and their estates, the profit was nowhere near what Henry VIII and Cromwell had initially hoped for. This was partly because of the expense of the foundation of six new dioceses using ex-monastic churches for their cathedrals and the provision of pensions for all evicted clergy. Cromwell eventually fell foul of Henry VIII's fickle sense of loyalty and he was executed in 1540 after his many enemies persuaded the king to believe the fatuous notion that he was a traitor. On the day of his execution Henry married Catherine Howard and soon afterwards went to war with Scotland and France and blew much of the monastic proceeds on short-term military expenses.

The real beneficiaries of the dissolution were the aristocracy and landed gentry (and occasionally very rich lawyers or merchants) who were able to buy the empty monasteries and their estates. The government, acting through a department specially set up for the purpose and called 'The Court of Augmentations', was careful about who acquired the properties: they were not put on the open market or auctioned, but interested parties could apply to make a purchase, and if considered suitable they might be successful. Priority was given to former patrons or benefactors of the monasteries, but most buyers were existing landowners who were very keen to increase the prestige and status of their families by acquiring manors which carried with them feudal obligations, considered highly desirable as a badge of social advancement.

The fate of Combe Abbey between 1539 and the 1580s is not known in great detail but we do know that the manors of Combe and Smite were granted by the crown almost immediately to Mary FitzRoy, the Duchess of Richmond, aged twenty. Born Lady Mary Howard, she was a daughter of the third Duke of Norfolk and first cousin to Queen Anne Boleyn and second cousin to Queen Catherine Howard. In 1533 she was married to Henry VIII's illegitimate son Henry FitzRoy, Duke of Richmond, but he died within three years, when they were both only seventeen. This was a disaster for everyone concerned because despite being illegitimate Fitzroy was considered a strong candidate to succeed his father on the throne in preference to his half-sisters Mary and Elizabeth. Henry did not permit Fitzroy's young widow to inherit all his properties but the grant of Combe Abbey and its estates went some way to providing an income for her. After the execution of Queen Catherine Howard in 1542 and the fall from grace of her family, Mary spent some time confined in the Tower but survived this and subsequent court intrigues. Rather a tragic figure, she never married again, lived quietly and died in 1557, aged 38.[1]

Until her death the Duchess of Richmond remained the ultimate owner of the Combe Abbey estate and her agents lost no time in capitalising on its potential income by leasing it to tenants. Almost immediately, parts of the land, though not the abbey buildings, were

The first owner of Combe Abbey after its dissolution in 1539 was Mary, (right) the young widow of Henry VIII's illegitimate son Henry, Duke of Richmond, (above), who died when they were both seventeen.

leased to Sir William Raynsford of Great Tew in Oxfordshire, some parts for sixty and some for forty years. In 1547 the reversion to the rest of the property (i.e the right to lease it until the death of the duchess) including the abbey buildings, was sold to the ambitious courtier John Dudley, who rose to a position of great power and influence under Henry VIII and Edward VI, acquiring the titles of Earl of Warwick and Duke of Northumberland. Dudley's crucial part in the events of the reign of the boy king Edward VI is well known – how he toppled his rival the Duke of Somerset and became Protector of the Realm, then married one of his younger sons to Lady Jane Grey and proclaimed her queen when Edward VI unexpectedly died, and then was executed for treason in 1553 when this plot failed and Henry VIII's elder daughter Mary was recognized as queen.

After Northumberland's execution the reversion to Combe Abbey passed to his son Viscount de L'Isle, but he died the following year. His widow inherited the reversion which passed to her second husband, Sir Edward Unton, who was in possession when the Duchess of Richmond eventually died in 1557. The duchess had therefore 'owned' the Combe estate for eighteen years but it is very unlikely that either she or the Dudleys had much to do with it personally. It is more probable that Sir William Raynesford was a 'hands on' tenant, responsible for either farming his part of the estate himself or letting it out to sub-tenants.[2] It is quite likely that during this period the abbey church was stripped of valuable materials, such as lead, but otherwise left to decay. Other parts of the monastery, such as the west range of the cloisters, seem to have been converted into domestic living quarters by the tenants at quite an early date.[3]

After the death of the duchess the manors of Combe and Smite returned to royal ownership and in 1559 they were leased for forty years to Robert Keilwey, Surveyor of the Courts of Wards and Liveries, at an annual rent of £196.[4] The Court had been set up (thanks to Cromwell) in 1540 and was a good example of Tudor administrative efficiency in that it was intended to maximise revenue from the crown's ancient rights over feudal taxes and also wardship: this was the crown's responsibility for the person and estates of heirs and heiresses aged under twenty-one. Keilwey, who was already in his mid-sixties, came from a gentry family based in Dorset and Hampshire. He trained as a lawyer and was admitted to the Inner Temple probably in the late 1520s, becoming a bencher in 1542. In 1545 he was recorder for Bristol and an MP for the city and he was an adviser to Edward Seymour, the Duke of Somerset, through whose influence he was appointed Surveyor of the Court of Wards in 1546. According to one of his biographers, 'It is a testimony to Keilwey's ability and moderation that he retained his office under four sovereigns, through various changes in religion and despite the fall of his patron Somerset in 1549'.[5]

One of Keilwey's great achievements, together with the politician Sir Walter Mildmay, was to ensure that the abolition of chantry funds did not lead to the collapse of the grammar schools, many of which were funded from this source. During the short reign of the boy king Keilwey and Mildmay were given responsibility for the foundation of several 'King Edward VI' grammar schools, a process which made a major contribution to the progress of general education in England. Keilwey married Cecily Bulstrode and they had only one child, a daughter named Anne. He became a JP for Berkshire in 1549 and probably lived with his family in that county until he was able to buy the lease on the Combe Abbey estate in 1559. He remained active in public administration, with houses in Fleet Street, London, and another in Stepney and he died in 1581 at the age of 84. He may have used part of the old abbey buildings as a residence for his family during this period, but he was buried in Exton parish church on the Rutland estate of his son-in-law's family where there is a fine monument to him complete with an effigy and inscription praising him as a distinguished lawyer.[6] This choice of resting place suggests that he had not built a significant new house at Combe.

Robert Keilwey (or Kelway) acquired Combe in 1559 and died in 1581. His elaborate tomb in the medieval parish church of St Peter and St Paul in Exton, Rutland, includes effigies of himself (top right) and his daughter and heiress Anne (bottom right). She and her husband Sir John (later Lord) Harington (bottom left) inherited much of his property, including Combe.

Lord Harington's new house, 1581-1605

When Keilwey died he left the whole of the Combe Abbey lands to his daughter, Anne, who was then aged thirty and already married to John Harington, some ten years her senior. He was the eldest son of Sir James Harington, the owner of one of the largest estates in Rutland, based on Exton Hall. John became a lawyer and entered the Inner Temple in 1558 at a time when Robert Keilwey was the Treasurer, so they came to know each other well. He represented Rutland as MP in 1571 and about the same time he married Anne Keilwey: no doubt her socially ambitious father had done nothing to prevent such a suitable match. When Keilwey died Harington inherited the Combe Abbey estate in right of his wife, and as his father was still very much alive and in possession of the Exton estate, he decided to build a grand house on the footprint of the former Combe Abbey. His father had been engaged for some years in the creation of a magnificent Elizabethan mansion at Exton Hall (sadly destroyed by fire in 1810) and no doubt this was an encouragement for his son to make his own mark at Combe.

It is the opinion of the architectural historian Warwick Rodwell that the west range of the cloister at Combe shows signs of having been converted to domestic use at some time between 1540 and 1580, so the task facing the Haringtons after they inherited Combe in 1581 was to demolish anything that remained of the abbey church and the south side of the cloister and to convert the west, north and east cloisters into a traditional Tudor-style house, no doubt making use of some of the stone from the ruined monastery buildings. A chimney-piece in the south-west wing of the completed house bore the Harington arms and the date 1590, so it is likely that the new mansion was finished by then. According to Rodwell:

> The three remaining cloister walks were retained as a
> corridor giving access to the ground floor rooms: they

An early drawing of the new mansion at Combe built by
Sir John Harington and probably completed around 1590.
The rectangular terrace in front of the house is where the
demolished abbey originally stood but the remodelled cloisters
remain, together with grand new apartments to the north,
surmounted by a cupola.

were entered from the courtyard at the south-east and south-west corners. There was no axial entrance. The monastic north range was demolished and rebuilt, with two large rooms lying parallel to the walk. Towards the west was the great hall with a lateral fireplace and north-facing windows, and to the east was a slightly smaller room which was probably the great chamber...[which] had a large east-facing mullioned and transomed window of twenty-eight lights. Demolished in 1863 the rich interior of what is thought to be this room was captured in an engraving published in the 1840s.[7]

In addition to all this there was a staircase wing with a large mullioned window which led to rooms above the hall and great chamber, and there were five rooms of equal size above both the east and west cloisters. At the southern ends of the east and west wings there were two pairs of Dutch-style gables which gave the house an impressive appearance when viewed from the south. The area where the abbey church had stood was cleared and made into a terrace, giving fine, south-facing vistas of the countryside beyond. The finished house was not a huge Elizabethan pile on the scale of Hatfield or Burghley, but it was very handsome and contained some fine interior carving and plaster decoration.

While the building work was in progress at Combe, Harington was a busy man elsewhere. By now he was the father of a son and two daughters and he served on the commission of the peace for Kesteven in Lincolnshire and he was a JP for Rutland and Warwickshire. In 1582/3 he served as High Sheriff of Warwickshire and he was knighted in 1584, no doubt through the influence of his patron, Robert Dudley, Earl of Leicester. The favourite of Elizabeth I, Leicester was one of the most influential men in England at the time and Harington served under him in the Netherlands campaign of 1585. The following year

Harington was MP for Warwickshire and he was among those who escorted Mary Queen of Scots through the county towards the end of that year on her journey to Fotheringhay Castle, where she was executed within a few months.

In 1592 Harington's father died and the social and financial status of Sir John was greatly enhanced when he inherited the Exton estate, with main seats at Exton and Burley, and he was appointed deputy-lieutenant of Rutland and Warwickshire. By the late 1590s he was considered to be among the richest knights in the kingdom, more wealthy than many members of the peerage, into which his daughter Lucy entered on her marriage to Edward Russell, the Earl of Bedford, in 1594. In 1589 Harington and the Earl of Kent were appointed executors of the will of Frances Sidney, widow of the Earl of Sussex, a relation of Harington's mother. The couple were childless and she left five thousand pounds and a quantity of silver plate with instructions that her executors should use this to found a new college at Cambridge, to be named Sidney Sussex College after her. Working together with Archbishop John Whitgift, Harington and Kent duly founded the college in 1596 on strict Protestant lines. The original E-shaped building stood on the footprint of the present college but was built of red brick which has been encased in stone by later architects. The college was built at about the same time as Harington was creating his house at Combe Abbey, though the college was much smaller: however, it has survived with distinction as one of the many jewels in Cambridge's crown and must be regarded as among Harington's most lasting achievements.

When Elizabeth I died in March, 1603, Harington lost no time in travelling up to York to pay homage to his new sovereign, Elizabeth's cousin King James VI of Scotland, and he accompanied him on his journey south, entertaining him to dinner at his house at Burley. At the same time his daughter, Lucy, Countess of Bedford, was one of the first to pay her respects to the new queen, Anne of Denmark, which marked the beginning of a close friendship. In June James's daughter Princess Elizabeth, nearly seven, stayed for four days at Combe with her entourage on her way down from Scotland to London and in the following month Harington was rewarded for these demonstrations of loyalty and support for James I by his elevation to the peerage as Baron Harington of Exton.[8]

The Gunpowder Plot, 1605

When Princess Elizabeth arrived in London she was at first placed under the charge of Lord and Lady Cobham but this rapidly changed when Cobham, a Roman Catholic, was implicated with his brother in two plots to replace James I, who was a Protestant, with his cousin Arabella Stuart, a Catholic. Cobham and Sir Walter Raleigh, who was also involved, were imprisoned for most of the rest of their lives and in October 1603 James decided to place his daughter in the care of Harington, who was known to be not only dependably loyal to himself, but also an enthusiastic Protestant. Accordingly, Princess Elizabeth and a considerable entourage of courtiers were accommodated at Combe Abbey, where she would spend five of the most formative years of her youth, from the ages of seven to twelve, in the care of Lord and Lady Harington. According to Elizabeth's biographer, Jessica Gorst-Williams:

> Combe Abbey was a beautiful place. Cloistered and surrounded by pastures and woodlands, it seemed to belong to a different age, away from the troubles of the present one. Oak and velvet dominated the furniture and beneath the large window of Elizabeth's bedroom were flowerbeds with a myriad of flowers. Stretching beyond were expanses of green and parkland, box hedges and lavender, bordering gravel paths.[9]

A youthful portrait of
Princess Elizabeth,
daughter of
King James I, seen
with her guardian,
Lord Harington.

Lord Harington (who should not be confused with his younger cousin and namesake Sir John Harington, the poet, author and alleged inventor of the flushing lavatory) was a man of considerable intellect and learning and was certainly regarded as a good and amusing teacher by his royal pupil. One of his particular interests was astronomy and he carefully explained the laws of Copernicus and instructed Elizabeth in the use his own telescope. Elizabeth's main academic tutor and chaplain was John Tovey, the master of the free school at Coventry and an uncompromising Protestant. A number of high-born girls were chosen as companions to the princess and one of these was Lord Harington's niece Ann Dudley, who became a great friend. The girls were schooled in history, geography, theology, natural history, music and foreign languages, at which Elizabeth became especially proficient. She was fond of animals and kept several as pets and also 'had an aviary built and a "fairy farm", stocked with miniature breeds of cattle and sheep from the isles of Shetland, Jersey and Man'.[10] She also persuaded Harington to build a small thatched cottage on an island in a lake in the park at Combe which would be the home of a poor widow and her children, whose main task was to look after the wild birds on the lake. When it was not possible to acquire a particular bird because it would not survive the climate, Harington had one stuffed and set up among the trees in its own wooden house.

The Cobham 'Bye' and 'Main' plots of 1603 proved only to be the precursor of one of the potentially most outrageous 'terrorist' atrocities in English history. The fireworks and fun of centuries of 'Bonfire Nights' have over the years tended to obscure the fact that the plot that was mercifully discovered in time on 5 November 1605 was intent on mass murder – the destruction of the king, his son and heir and the vast majority of the nobility and gentry of England in one colossal explosion, when they were all assembled together in the House of Lords for the ceremonial opening of Parliament.

After Henry VIII's renunciation of papal authority the

Chapter Two

Protestant Reformation in England had made steady progress, emboldened by the brief reign of the unpopular Catholic Queen Mary, who had attempted to restore Catholicism and notoriously burned prominent Protestants at the stake. Her sister Elizabeth I, reared a Protestant, proceeded cautiously until the Catholic King Philip II of Spain declared war and sent 'the Spanish Armada' to invade England in 1588. He had been the husband of Mary Tudor and was recognized as titular king during her reign so his intention was to capture Elizabeth and take the throne himself, a dire threat to English national sovereignty as well as the Protestant religion. After the defeat of the Armada strict legislation against Catholics was enforced: Catholic priests were banned in England and Catholics who refused to attend Protestant services were considered as 'recusants' and fined heavily.

The 'Gunpowder Plot' was hatched by Robert Catesby, the only surviving son of Sir William Catesby, a member of a long-established family of Warwickshire gentry, some of whom had been tenants of Combe Abbey in the fifteenth century. His mother was Anne Throckmorton of Coughton Court in Alcester and both his parents were prominent 'recusant' Catholics. In 1593, when he was about twenty-one, Catesby married Catherine, the daughter of Sir Thomas Leigh, whose family had acquired Stoneleigh Abbey in 1558. She was not a Catholic but she died five years later, after which Catesby's Catholic views became extreme to the point of unhinged fanaticism and in 1601 he supported the Earl of Essex's rebellion against Elizabeth I, hoping to replace her with a monarch more favourable to Catholics. The plot failed, Essex was executed and Catesby, though spared, was fined a huge sum of money (4,000 marks) – several millions of pounds today.[11]

Many Catholics hoped that James I would be tolerant towards them: after all, his mother, Mary Queen of Scots, had been a lifelong Catholic. But he had been raised as a Protestant, had married Anne, a daughter of the Protestant king of Denmark, and brought up their children, Henry, Elizabeth and Charles, as Protestants. Moreover, after the 'Bye' and 'Main' plots his attitude to Catholics hardened and he ordered that the existing legislation against them should be strictly enforced. Catesby therefore came to the conclusion that the most drastic action was justified and early in 1604 he began to recruit sympathisers to plan the destruction, not only of the king, but of the entire Protestant establishment. The first recruits were his friend Thomas Percy, a junior member of the famous Northumberland family, his cousin the lawyer Thomas Wintour, John Wright, an excellent swordsman, and Guido or Guy Fawkes, a soldier very experienced in the use of explosives. By May they had decided to blow up the House of Lords at the next ceremonial opening of Parliament, when the royal family, peers of the realm and MPs would all be present. To this end they recruited eight more conspirators, including a young and rather dashing landowner, Sir Everard Digby.

With the king and his heir, Prince Henry, dead, the plotters intended to place on the throne his daughter Princess Elizabeth, who at that time was at Combe Abbey in the charge of Lord and Lady Harington, and of course totally unaware of the plot. It was agreed that she would be kidnapped and a scheme was worked out by which Digby would assemble a group of supporters, pretending to be a hunting party, on Dunsmore Heath, a few miles from Combe, and they would seize her after the destruction of the king. The plotters regarded Elizabeth, then aged nine, as the ideal candidate because not only did a French ambassador describe her as tall for her age, well-bred and handsome, but she had already made a good impression on folk in the Midlands when Harington took her from Combe to Coventry in April 1604, where she was entertained by the city authorities. After visiting the free school and presenting it with some books, she attended a civic service in the impressive parish church of St Michael, with its magnificent spire, and then 'sat solemnly beneath a canopy of state in St Mary's Hall and [ate] a solitary dinner, watched by neighbouring

The Gunpowder plotters of 1605. Robert Catesby and Guido (or Guy) Fawkes are second and third from the right.

dignitaries.' As Antonia Fraser points out in her history of the Gunpowder Plot:

> The princess was therefore far from being an unknown
> quantity to those who lived locally – as [royal persons]
> might otherwise be in an age without newspapers. On
> the contrary, the conspirators knew that she could fulfil
> a ceremonial role despite her comparative youth.[12]

As is well known, a warning letter, which may or may not have been a fake, was sent to a peer, Lord Monteagle, who immediately took it to Robert Cecil, the king's chief minister. A subsequent search of the undercroft beneath the then House of Lords (not the building of today, which was constructed after the devastating fire of 1834) revealed around midnight on 4 November no less than 36 barrels of gunpowder with Guy Fawkes standing ready to light the fuse at the appropriate moment. In 2005 a replica of the building was constructed for a TV programme and blown up with a similar quantity of gunpowder: the result was a huge explosion leaving only a pile of rubble, establishing beyond doubt that had the plot succeeded the House of Lords would have been demolished and everyone trapped within it would have been killed.[13]

Lord Harington was informed on November 6 that a number of horses had been stolen from Warwick Castle and suspecting that trouble was afoot he immediately had Princess Elizabeth escorted to the safety of Coventry. There 'she lodged with a Mr Hopkins of Palace Yard, off the High Street. The Mayor, Mr Collyns, and nine other citizens mounted guard, drawing bows, pikes, blackbills, corslets, partisans, halberds and gloves from the city armoury for this purpose.'[14] This was a wise move, because as soon as they heard that Fawkes had been arrested Catesby and his associates rode hard from London to meet up with Digby at Dunwich where Catesby, clearly having lost touch with reality, lied to Digby, saying that the plot had succeeded, the king was dead and they must raise a revolt among local Catholic families. They rode to Combe only to find that Princess Elizabeth had gone and pursued by loyal forces they eventually reached Holbeche House in Staffordshire and foolishly attempted to dry out some damp gunpowder they had brought with them. It exploded and Catesby and others were badly injured.

The Sheriff of Worcestershire and 200 men surrounded the house on 8 November and Catesby and some of his henchmen were killed and the rest taken prisoner. The plotters who survived, including Fawkes and Digby, were subsequently tried, found guilty of high treason and condemned to the full penalty of being hanged, castrated, disembowelled and their bodies hacked into four pieces. Without exception they accepted their fate with fortitude and died proud Catholics. Meanwhile Princess Elizabeth, naturally shocked by the whole episode and the role the plotters had mapped out for her, said to Harington 'What a queen should I have been by this means? I had rather have been with my royal father in Parliament House than wear his crown on such conditions'. The wicked plot to kill her father and her beloved older brother Henry was all that she and her friends at Combe Abbey talked about for several months afterwards.[15]

The Harington family at Court, 1608-1613

The household of Princess Elizabeth at Combe was by no means small, numbering some 141 'courtiers' and 85 servants. Moreover, both the king and Prince Henry came to visit her from time to time and on these occasions Lord Harington's expenses for their entertainment must have been colossal. It seems that the king had agreed to pay him two thousand pounds a year to look after his daughter but James's shortage of money and tendency to be mean was notorious. Elizabeth, however, was generous to a fault:

> By the time Elizabeth was twelve she was fluent in several languages and imbued with a thorough understanding of the Protestant religion. She was not very musical and she did not enjoy needlework. However, she was an excellent rider and her knowledge did justice to the fact that she was the daughter of the professedly most learned king in Christendom. Already, she was amusing and easily amused; popular, and, unlike her father, very generous. It was this generosity which stopped her, in Lord Harington's eyes, from being the ideal princess. She did not seem to comprehend the rudiments of domestic finance. She enjoyed giving presents and was quite unable to control her personal expenditure. Having found employment for various local people and financed them with her own allowance, she now wanted to start a school to educate local children. It was quite out of the question, Lord Harington told her; where was the money to come from?...When Lord Harington scolded her for overspending, Elizabeth would burst into a flood of repentant tears and do it again. When King James came to see her it would be her lack of thrift for which he criticised her.[16]

Around the time of Elizabeth's residence at Combe Harington made a few changes to the house. The south fronts of the east and west wings, formerly of brick, were embellished with handsome mullioned and transomed windows in stone with ogee-style gables while an ornately carved porch with fan vaulting was built on the eastern side

Around the time of Princess Elizabeth's residence at Combe (1603-8) Lord Harington made grand additions to the house including an entrance porch (top) and a magnificent reception room (below) both of which were adorned with very fine carving, possibly by the famous Inigo Jones.
From drawings by J.G. Jackson, c 1846.

An allegorical group portrait of the family of James I (wearing his crown), with his wife, Queen Anne, on his right and the next heir, Prince Charles, in front. To the right of the picture can be seen Elizabeth and Frederick (with the crown of Bohemia suspended by a cherub) and many of their children.

of the east range, leading from the gallery on that side of the house down to a walled garden. The famous sculptor Inigo Jones worked on the house at this time, with a small army of craftsmen, and it is likely that it was he who was responsible for the decoration of the great chamber which was described later as 'the great dining-room where the best carving is'.[17]

Inevitably, as she grew older, Elizabeth grew restless with her relatively quiet routine at Combe and in 1608, aged twelve, she successfully persuaded her father to allow her to take part in the life of the royal court. She was provided with rooms in Whitehall Palace in London and at Hampton Court but she remained under the tutelage of Lord and Lady Harington and spent a good deal of her time in their house at Kew. As guardians of the princess the Haringtons were naturally given an honoured and influential place at court, but their children Lucy and John were also making a mark in their own right.

Lucy was born in 1580 and at the age of thirteen she married the Earl of Bedford, then aged 22. As a result of the friendship she developed with Queen Anne she was appointed a lady of the bedchamber and was an influential patron of writers such as Ben Jonson and John Donne as well as many less well-known poets, dramatists and musicians. Despite being a committed Calvinist, she performed and also directed court masques and was renowned for her beauty and intellect. Her much younger and only brother, John, born in 1592, grew up to be one of the most admired young men of his generation. Through the princess he came to know Prince Henry and a close friendship developed between the two. In 1604 (aged twelve) he was made a Knight of the Bath and he became an official companion of the Prince of Wales, (aged ten). John spent a year studying at the new Sidney Sussex College at Cambridge from 1607 to 1608 then went on a grand tour of the continent in the company of a number of companions, including his tutor, John Tovey, the schoolmaster from Coventry.[18]

During his absence of eighteen months John Harington acted as a roving ambassador for Prince Henry, feeding the heir apparent with information about the countries and rulers he met and the prevailing political and diplomatic issues. He travelled to Brussels, Heidelberg, Florence and Venice, where the British ambassador voiced the opinion that 'being the right eye of the Prince of Wales, this world holds that [Harington] will one day govern the kingdom'. He spent six months in Venice, studying the republic and its constitution before moving on to Vienna, Prague and Paris. Shortly after his return to England he was returned as MP for Coventry in the summer of 1609. He was still only seventeen.

All was set for the Haringtons to become the mainstay of the new Stuart dynasty, with Lord Harington the much loved and respected guardian of Princess Elizabeth, his daughter Lucy the main confidante of the Queen and his son John the best friend of the Prince of Wales. Now that Princess Elizabeth was making regular appearances at court, her beauty and attractive personality was much reported on by foreign ambassadors and James I began to receive enthusiastic enquiries from foreign rulers seeking a suitable wife. These included the kings of Sweden and Spain, the heir to the throne of France and Frederick V, the Elector Palatine, hereditary ruler of extensive lands in Germany. Unlike the others he could not offer Elizabeth the status of a queen, but he was the same age as she was and he was a Calvinist, whereas the others were mostly Catholics and James I was well aware that the marriage of his daughter to a Catholic would not be popular in England or Scotland. Frederick himself was very keen on the match and he arrived in England on 16 October 1612 and met Elizabeth for the first time. He was not disappointed; neither was she and their relationship soon developed into a love match.

But within three weeks of their meeting, everything at the Stuart court was thrown into confusion by the devastating blow of the death of the Prince of Wales. He had complained of various aches and pains all year but he was so young and fit that no great importance had been attached to them. In October he caught a chill which developed complications and he died on 6 November, aged 18. Unlike his father or his weakly younger brother, Charles, he was hugely popular and the nation was plunged into mourning. Elizabeth, who loved him deeply, was inconsolable. Moreover, his death meant that only the insecure life of her younger brother Charles, aged twelve, now stood between her and the throne. The marriage negotiations, in which Lord Harington played a significant part, stalled for a time but eventually James I committed himself to the match and the couple were married on St Valentine's Day 1613 in the royal chapel in Whitehall Palace, with Lady Harington escorting the bride down the aisle.

Well aware that the allowance that James I theoretically paid to Harington to defray the expenses of maintaining Elizabeth was far less than the actual costs he bore – including some aspects of the wedding – Elizabeth persuaded her father to grant him a monopoly over the right to coin brass farthings (which became known as 'Haringtons') in an attempt to defray his debts, which were said to stand at £30,000. When Frederick and Elizabeth set sail for Germany in April both the Haringtons went with them in charge of her considerable retinue of English courtiers. Though appreciated for her charm and beauty, Elizabeth remained disorganized in financial matters and Harington had problems in maintaining order among the English members of her household. Moreover, James I insisted that Elizabeth's royal rank should be recognized by her husband and his family at all times – after all, she would become Queen of England and Scotland should the boy Charles die – and this created tensions over questions of precedence at the Heidelberg court. On the other hand, the match elevated Frederick's status among the princes of Germany and strengthened the cause of Protestantism on the continent. Moreover, Frederick and Elizabeth remained very happy together and Elizabeth eventually bore him eight boys and five girls.[19]

After three months in Heidelberg, the Haringtons took their leave of the young woman they had more or less raised since the age of seven and began their journey home but at Worms Lord Harington fell ill of a fever. He died on 23 August, aged 73, and his body was taken back to Exton for burial. Despite his annual income of between five and seven thousand pounds, Harington died heavily in debt and the burden of these fell upon his heir, John, who now became the second baron. The death of his friend Prince Henry the previous year had been a major blow to his prospects, but he now turned to tackle the considerable responsibilities of running the estates at Exton and Combe, and of taking his place in the House of Lords. Within six months, however, he contracted the dreaded smallpox, which killed him in February 1614 at the age of 22. He died unmarried and was buried with his father at Exton, mourned by all as a fine young man, a model of puritan piety and, as John Donne put it, one who 'dids't intrude on death, usurps't a grave'. [20]

This was a double disaster because the barony became extinct and faced with demanding creditors, the family was forced to sell the Exton estate to a rich London merchant, Sir Baptist Hicks. He was later created a peer as Viscount Camden, a title remaindered to his son-in-law, Edward Noel, whose descendants still own the estate. The rest of the Harington property was divided between the two remaining daughters, Lucy Countess of Bedford, who inherited two thirds, and Frances, Lady Chichester, a third. The Combe Abbey estate was part of Lucy Bedford's inheritance, and she owned it for the next eight years. As well as being a notable figure at the court of James I and an enthusiastic patron of the arts, she was also very interested in architecture and garden design. In 1608 she acquired Twickenham Park House, near Richmond, and after spending time and money on its improvement she eventually gave it to her relative Sir William Harington. In 1616 she decided to lease Combe Abbey to young George Villiers, the dazzlingly handsome young favourite whom

James I had just knighted and would eventually create Duke of Buckingham. Whether he made much use of Combe we do not know, but it is doubtful. Meanwhile, Lucy and her husband embarked upon the building of a fine new house at Moor Park in Hertfordshire, which swallowed up even more of their money. Lucy was also an enthusiastic gambler and in 1622 it seems that she was forced to sell Combe Abbey to cover her losses: both she and her husband died in 1627, leaving no children and alleged debts of £50,000.[21]

The Haringtons were certainly not a dull family, being ambitious, imaginative and intellectually gifted. But they were over-generous to the point of prodigality, many of their achievements evaporated and they are remembered less than, perhaps, they deserve. Even at Combe today little remains of John Harington's original Elizabethan house except for the outline of the cloisters and part of the west wing.

Chapter Three

The Cavalier Earl

Lord Craven and the Queen of Bohemia

For the considerable sum of £36,000 Lucy Bedford sold the Combe Abbey estate to Elizabeth, Lady Craven, the widow of one of the most remarkable mercantile success stories in Tudor England. Sir William Craven was one of the best-known 'tycoons' of his day: he started life around 1545 as the son of very unpretentious parents who lived at Burnsall, near Skipton in Yorkshire and as a boy he was apprenticed to Robert Hulson, a London merchant. He had a natural genius for business recognized by Hulson and also Robert Parker, who became a partner in his enterprises which centred initially on the wholesaling of cloth to home markets and later moneylending on a grand scale, to the crown as well as many grandees. After 1588 his business was conducted from a huge mansion in Watling Street and in 1603 he provided cloth worth £600 for the funeral of Queen Elizabeth. He was one of the many people knighted by James I soon after his accession and from 1607 he lived in 'Zouche's Inn' on Leadenhall Street, a vast house with sixty-two rooms which later became the headquarters of the East India Company.

From 1582 onwards Craven was very much involved in the civic politics of the City of London, of which he was Lord Mayor in 1610/11. He was committed to a godly life according to the Protestant religion and he founded a grammar school near his birthplace at Burnsall in 1605 and was a generous benefactor of Christ's Hospital in London and St John's College Oxford, as well as several City churches. Around 1597, when he was fifty, he married Elizabeth

Sir William Craven (1545-1618) was probably the most famous rags-to-riches story of his generation. He made a huge fortune as a London merchant and financier, the bulk of which went to his elder son, who became the first Earl of Craven. Portrait after Marcus Gheeraerts the Younger.

A portrait of the youthful Frederick V, Elector Palatine, whose
marriage to Princess Elizabeth was a love-match. Below is a
contemporary view of his palace at Heidelberg Castle,
overlooking the Rhine.

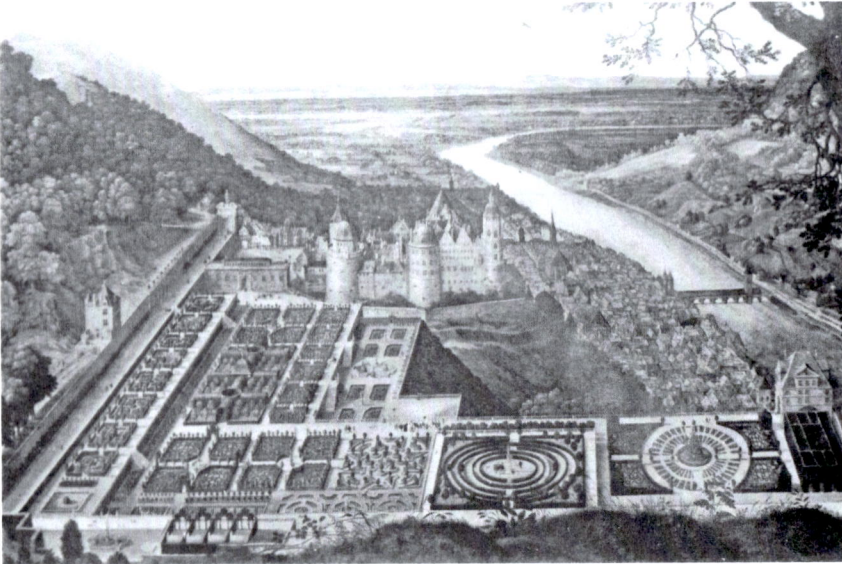

Whitmore, from another merchant family in the City and she bore him four sons and three daughters. When he died in 1618 he was worth at least £125,000. It is notoriously difficult to convert historic values into present day currency but he was almost certainly what we would today call a 'billionaire'.[1]

Craven's will contained a fair number of generous benefactions, but the bulk of his money passed to his widow. He had not himself invested in land, presumably because he needed capital for his money-lending enterprises, but his will instructed his widow to put the family fortune into landed estates. In 1620 Stokesay Castle in Shropshire, with about five thousand acres, was acquired for £13,500, and the house and estate at Hamstead Marshall, Berks, in the same year. Combe Abbey followed in 1622, while houses and estates at Caversham near Reading and Benham Valence, near Newbury, were also added to the list. When Lady Craven died two years later, reputed to be the richest widow who ever died in London, she left £8,000 a year to her elder surviving son, William, and £5,000 to the younger, John. Two of her daughters, meanwhile, married peers, Lord Powis and Lord Coventry. The elder son, William, received the bulk of the family fortune which included properties in London and the estates of Combe Abbey, Hamstead Marshall, Stokesay Castle and Caversham Park, as well as other lands, manors and houses in Oxfordshire, Somerset and Sussex.

At the time of his inheritance William Craven was sixteen years old and he had already spent a year studying at Trinity College, Oxford. Now a very rich young man he gave up his academic studies in favour of an active career as a soldier in the Protestant army of Prince Maurice of Nassau, the 'stadhouder' or elected ruler of many Dutch provinces. Maurice, an elderly but very experienced general, was fighting against the Catholic Habsburg Ferdinand II, Holy Roman Emperor of Germany, in an attempt to rescue his nephew the Prince of the Palatinate and his wife Elizabeth from the disaster that had overtaken them soon after their marriage. In August 1619 the Protestant Parliament of Bohemia rebelled against Ferdinand as their ruler and offered the throne to Frederick. Against the advice of James I and many other European rulers, Frederick accepted, well aware that this was bound to lead to war with Ferdinand. Frederick and Elizabeth were crowned in Prague on 4 November 1619 but their brief reign ended when the Bohemians were defeated by Ferdinand's forces in an hour-long engagement outside Prague on 8 November 1620, known as the 'Battle of the White Mountain'.

Frederick and Elizabeth were forced to flee to the Netherlands while Bohemia as well as Frederick's Palatinate were seized from him by the Habsburgs. Many blamed Elizabeth for urging her husband to risk so much for regal status and their short reign led to them being known unflatteringly as the 'Winter King' and the 'Winter Queen'. James I was furious because he had considered the whole escapade foolish and dangerous. Moreover, he was now under pressure to send troops to the aid of his son-in-law and his entire policy as king so far had been to avoid war and especially the expense of it. However, his son Charles and his favourite, Buckingham, who had both been humiliated in Spain when they went to negotiate for a Spanish marriage for Charles, both demanded war against the Catholics, which was popular with parliament and the nation at large, so James reluctantly declared war on Spain in 1624.

It is surely not surprising that young William Craven was motivated to travel to the Netherlands to lend his support to the exiled Frederick and Elizabeth. He had just inherited an immense fortune and was therefore in a strong position to equip himself and a suitable retinue for the adventure. Moreover, he had been brought up to be a committed Protestant by his parents and Frederick was the leader of the Protestants in Germany. Craven's participation in the fighting was also a way of bringing himself to the notice of the people who mattered in England

and abroad, while finally he was now the owner of Combe Abbey, which he knew was dear to the heart of the exiled Queen of Bohemia.

It seems that Craven served with distinction in Maurice of Nassau's army but it was an inglorious period in the career of this notable general because in July 1624 the Spanish (who were allies of the Emperor) besieged the town of Breda, the headquarters of the Nassau family, and Maurice died in April 1625 with the town still under siege: it was forced to surrender two months later and this marked a major setback in the conflict between the Catholics and Protestants. The war had now been under way for seven years, with much devastation of property and loss of life in Bohemia, the Palatinate and other Protestant countries. Maurice was succeeded by his younger half-brother Frederick Henry of Orange, under whom Craven continued to serve for a year or so. James I died in March 1625 and his son Charles I succeeded him, relying strongly on the advice of Buckingham. They needed money for their war plans against Spain and when Craven returned to England full of honour for his attempt to defend the cause of Charles I's sister it is not surprising that the king not only knighted him on 4 March 1627 but eight days later, in return for Craven's useful 'gift' of £7,000, he created him Baron Craven of Hamstead Marshall.

This village in Berkshire was centred on a medieval castle which was once in the possession of the famous twelfth century warrior William the Marshal, after whom it was named. The manor had several distinguished owners until its purchase by Lady Craven in 1620 as part of her policy of investment in land, and there was a sizeable house there which it seems was considered the main Craven seat, rather than Combe Abbey. The new Lord Craven was clearly held in high regard by Charles I because he was appointed a member of the king's permanent council of war and in 1629 it was rumoured that he might marry a daughter of the Earl of Devonshire. Nothing came of this and in the same year Craven travelled to the

Netherlands, where he became dangerously ill, though he managed to recover.

Craven must be considered an unusual and eccentric person, so generous with his great wealth and loyal to his friends that even they considered him naïve and tended to make fun of him. Yet he was clearly a genuinely charitable soul, as is shown by the fact that in 1630 he spent £3,000 of his own money in order to release poor debtors from prisons in London, though he was also prepared to spend a great deal more that year in acquiring the fine house and estate at Benham Valence, near Newbury. In 1631 he received a commission from Charles I to serve as an officer in a small army which was sent to the aid of Prince Frederick and early in 1632 he was with Frederick when he linked forces with his Protestant ally Gustavus Adolphus, the famous warrior king of Sweden. Craven was wounded in subsequent fighting and won the respect of Gustavus for his bravery: he even offered to finance an independent army of his own to assist him but the Swedish king declined. Soon after this the Protestant cause in Germany was dealt a severe blow in November 1632 at the battle of Lützen which was a victory for the army of Gustavus, but he was killed on the battlefield. A further blow was the death of Frederick who died of the plague a few days later leaving an heir, Charles Louis, who was only fifteen.

By the summer of 1633 Craven was back in England, serving on the king's council in Wales and offering to provide security for a loan of £31,000 to Elizabeth and her son – though this fell through. Charles I's gratitude for his loyalty came in the form of a royal licence to enclose 600 acres of land round Combe Abbey to create a private park, which suggests that Craven used the house at times for his own occupation and was keen to improve its dignity and privacy. In 1636 he attempted unsuccessfully to stand surety for another loan of £30,000 for Elizabeth and his contemporaries were clearly puzzled as to why he was prepared to risk his own money in this way: Sir Ralph

William, first baron and first Earl of Craven (1608-1697), after Gerritt van Honthorst. Enormously rich, thanks to his father, he was an active soldier who fought tenaciously in the Protestant cause and came to be the defender and some thought the lover of Elizabeth, the widowed Queen of Bohemia. He was also a notable house builder, creating mansions at Caversham, Ashdown, Hamstead Marshall and Craven House in London. Combe Abbey was transformed during his lifetime by a series of additions, most notably a magnificent west wing built to designs by William Winde in the late 1680s.

Verney wrote that Craven was 'the subject of every man's discourse' for 'prodigality' and even 'folly'.[2]

Craven personally went into action again in 1637, lending Charles Louis £10,000 and joining a small force under him and his dashing younger brother, Prince Rupert, which marched up the Rhine and attempted to support their Swedish allies. But they were surrounded by Habsburg forces and Rupert and Craven were taken prisoner. Craven bought his own freedom for £20,000 in 1639 and offered to ransom Rupert but without success and he remained in captivity for some time longer. Craven returned to London and supported Charles Louis in asking Charles I to give more help. But the king, who had governed England without calling parliament since 1629, was facing social unrest at home and had massive financial as well as political problems. As these worsened and the Civil War began in 1642 Craven chose to live with Elizabeth and Charles Louis in Holland and remained there for the next eighteen years. For the first ten of these years his estates in England were run by his agents who managed and sub-let them to maximise their potential income.

Like many people in England during the Civil War period, Craven was torn in his loyalties. On the one hand he was a committed Protestant, sympathetic to some of the aims of the 'Roundheads'. On the other hand, he was a loyal servant of the crown and of Princess Elizabeth in particular. He decided to stay out of the fighting, though Elizabeth's son Prince Rupert was appointed Charles I's cavalry commander, experiencing initial success at the battle of Edgehill in 1642 before making fatal misjudgements at Marston Moor in 1644. After the royalist defeat at Naseby in 1645 Charles I's cause was effectively lost and Elizabeth and her family could only watch in horror from the Hague as the crisis deteriorated and her brother was beheaded in January 1649. Parliament abolished both the monarchy and the House of Lords and proclaimed the 'Commonwealth', soon to be dominated by Oliver Cromwell. Elizabeth ceased to receive a pension from England and Craven stepped in to help with her finances and tried (unsuccessfully) to arrange a marriage between her youngest daughter, Sophie, of whom he was very fond, and Charles I's son, recognized as Charles II by European courts. It has been calculated that in total Craven's financial assistance to the royalist cause up to 1660 amounted to £50,000.[3]

The Commonwealth government was in dire need of funds and one of its main policies was to confiscate the property of committed royalists. Early in 1651 evidence was put before the Council of State that Craven had given substantial help to 'Charles II', which was true enough, and it ordered the seizure of all his estates in Warwickshire, Shropshire, Sussex, Oxfordshire, Middlesex, Herefordshire, Gloucestershire and London. Parliament endorsed this decision in March and over the next year agents visited all the Craven properties, assessing their value and in some cases felling trees to raise immediate cash. In 1652 the decision was taken to sell all Craven's property to help finance a war against the Dutch, and although agents for Craven were allowed to argue the case against this drastic action, it was sanctioned by Parliament though the Bill passed by a narrow majority of only three votes.

Craven did not allow the matter to rest there and in 1654 a pamphlet was produced entitled 'The Lord Craven's Case Briefly Stated' which argued that he had been punished with undue severity at the hands of men eager to acquire his lands and property for their own gain. Cromwell, always a fair man up to a point, reviewed his case but took no action, and the sale of many of Craven's properties went ahead. The curtain wall at Stokesay Castle had already been demolished and in June 1654 the diarist John Evelyn recorded that he had seen Craven's house at Caversham, near Reading, in ruins with the woods all round it cut down.[4] Combe Abbey appears to have survived intact and this may be connected with the fact that the son of Craven's first cousin had married the daughter of Lord Fairfax, formerly Parliament's commander-in-chief. So during the interregnum

Combe was probably leased by the government to tenants who looked after it with a considerable degree of care.

While Craven's affairs in England suffered badly from the defeat of the royalists in the Civil War, the fortunes of Elizabeth's eldest son Charles Louis were improved when the Peace of Westphalia in 1648 finally concluded the disastrous conflict which has since become known as the 'Thirty Years War'. The Catholics failed in their ultimate objective to destroy Protestantism because it was agreed in 1648 that the ruler of each state would have the right to determine its religion, which might be Catholic, Lutheran or Calvinist. Spain recognized its former colonies in the Netherlands as an independent Dutch republic and Sweden made territorial gains in North Germany. As for the Palatinate, which had always been geographically divided, Charles Louis was restored to the Lower Palatinate, his ancestral lands along the Rhine based on Heidelberg, but he lost the Upper Palatinate to the Catholic Duke of Bavaria. As far as the wider European balance of power was concerned, the war resulted in a reduction of the influence of the Habsburg rulers of Spain and Germany and an increase in the power of the Bourbon rulers of France.

Charles Louis returned from exile in Holland in October 1649 to reclaim the Lower Palatinate where the pre-war population had been drastically reduced and Heidelberg Castle was mostly in ruins. He soon married and concentrated on the task in hand of restoring prosperity to his people and raising a family while his mother remained in the Wassaenor Hof in the Hague, her less than palatial residence, badly maintained because of lack of funds. Charles Louis, whose sympathies had generally been with Parliament in the English Civil War, was not on the best of terms with his mother and proved reluctant to release properties and estates legally due to her in the Palatinate, resulting in frequent quarrels between them over money. While her daughters Elizabeth and Sophia moved to Heidelberg Elizabeth could not afford to do so and still relied heavily on the financial and moral support of Craven to whom she wrote about this time:

A later portrait of the first Earl of Craven
by Sir Anthony van Dyke.

It may be that my next letter will tell you that I have no
more to eat: that is no parable, but the certain truth, for
there is no money nor credit of any; and this week if
there be none found, I shall have neither meat nor
candles'.[5]

But even Craven was not able to help as much as before after
the sequestration of his English estates, though he remained based in
the Hague for most of the 1650s. Of Elizabeth's thirteen children,
seven were dead by the middle of the decade and only one, Louise,
lived with her until 1657 when she shocked her mother to the core by
converting to Catholicism, as had two more of her children. The
youngest daughter, Sophia, eventually married the younger son of the
Duke of Brunswick, a match Elizabeth thought below her dignity: yet
as the dice strangely fell, their son George eventually became the first
Hanoverian king of Great Britain. Prince Rupert, who settled in the
Netherlands after years spent privateering against Commonwealth
vessels, was closest to his mother, though not a reliable source of
income. She was really kept afloat, both financially and in morale, by
the continued support of Lord Craven.

Inevitably the real nature of their relationship puzzled their
contemporaries and still intrigues people today. Were they physically
lovers? Suggestions that they were secretly married at some point in
the 1650s are impossible to prove one way or the other but it seems
very unlikely. Elizabeth's biographer Jessica Gorst-Williams gives no
credence to the notion:

Deeply in love with Elizabeth, who was considerably
older than he was, he longed to excel in wit and wisdom
and to win her admiration. Elizabeth in return was
grateful to him for his generosity, but that was all.[6]

Elizabeth, the widowed Queen of Bohemia, (1596-1662) by her favourite painter, Gerritt van Honthorst. Was she ever the lover, or even secretly the wife, of the first Earl of Craven?

Twelve years Craven's senior, Elizabeth was very conscious of her royal dignity and status as both the daughter of a king and the wife of a king. He, though very rich, handsome, valiant and a peer (though not very tall) was, in a very class-conscious world, still the son of a self-made merchant. Moreover, any suggestion that he was carrying on an affair with Elizabeth would be fraught with danger: in the late 1640s a young French nobleman boasted in the Hague, whether truthfully or not, of his successful liaisons with both Elizabeth and her daughter Louise and was stabbed to death in revenge by her son Philip.[7]

Yet there must have been a very considerable degree of infatuation with Elizabeth on Craven's part to have prevented him – one of the most eligible men in Britain – from finding a wife elsewhere. Also, given that he was an experienced professional soldier, it is surprising that he chose to remain with her in Holland and take no part in the English Civil War. So it must have been infatuation, or devotion, or indeed 'love', which kept him at Elizabeth's side - perhaps tempered with the advantages of 'social climbing': Craven's sponsorship of Elizabeth and her cause put him at the centre of royal circles, even if many smiled at his excessive generosity. But he was an exceptionally rich man: no doubt he felt that if it pleased him to be generous, he could easily afford to be.

The interregnum in Britain came to an end soon after the death of Oliver Cromwell in 1658 made it clear that there was no-one who could successfully fill his place except a monarch, so Elizabeth's nephew Charles II was restored to the throne in May 1660. Royalist property that had been confiscated was mostly returned to its owners and Lord Craven recovered the vast majority of his previous possessions, including Combe Abbey. Elizabeth had long since given up ideas of returning to Heidelberg and hoped that Charles II would invite her to England, perhaps with a suitable pension. When this did not happen and she was not even invited to his coronation, she relied again on the hospitality of Craven, who put at her disposal his large London house in Drury Lane. She arrived in May 1661 and was courteously received by Charles II who granted her proper precedence as a queen and escorted her to the opera and other entertainments. At the beginning of February 1662 she moved to a home of her own at Leicester House but within days she died of acute bronchitis and was buried with due pomp in Westminster Abbey, aged sixty-six, with her faithful Craven as the bearer of her crown.

Craven the builder

Once restored to his estates and income after the Restoration, Craven seems to have lost no time in implementing grand building projects. His house at Caversham Park, an Elizabethan manor which had been badly damaged after its sequestration, was demolished and a fine new house built to designs by William Winde. It seems that as early as 1661 Craven also decided to build a far grander house than the existing one at Hamstead Marshall and to build a completely new one in the Dutch style on his manor of Ashdown, near Ashbury, in what was then Berkshire (since 1974 Oxfordshire).

The new house at Ashdown turned out to be a very unusual building to find in the English countryside. It was three storeys tall with an attic storey surmounted by a cupola and golden ball and because it was only five windows wide it had the appearance of a doll's house, though flanking pavilions on either side lent it some degree of grandeur. Indoors, many of the rooms were originally panelled and there was a fine staircase leading to a platform on the roof from which there are magnificent views of the Berkshire Downs. It is thought likely that William Winde was the architect and scholars have pointed to similarities with the Chateau de Balleroy in Normandy and also designs published in Rubens's *Palazzi di Genova*, which was printed in English

Ashdown House, near Ashbury, Oxfordshire, built for the first
Earl of Craven and completed about 1665.

in 1662, though the main impression given is of a house in the Dutch style of domestic architecture.[8] Either way, it was a unique house of considerable attraction, destined to become a favourite residence of the Cravens in future years.

It is possible that Ashdown was originally conceived so that Elizabeth of Bohemia might have a suitable residence to occupy when she was in England and the novelist Nicola Cornick produced in 2016 a historical romance entitled 'House of Shadows', suggesting that it was intended as a gift to her, with gardens designed as love-tokens. Cornick did some serious historical research for the book, including reading letters from Craven to Elizabeth which, she writes, 'give a fascinating insight into their relationship, on her part demonstrating her complete trust in him and on his, showing a very respectful admiration'.[9] As we know, whether Elizabeth ever allowed this 'respectful admiration' to develop into consummated love remains a much-debated question. Ashdown House was still on the drawing-board when Elizabeth died: why, therefore, did Craven go ahead with the building of it, which took several years? Perhaps he saw it as a memorial, a hunting lodge which he could use from time to time and ponder past moments spent with his 'Winter Queen'.

Craven's decision to build a new house at Hamstead Marshall seems more straightforward. He may well have considered that in the extravagant mood of Restoration England it was appropriate for someone of his status to be the owner of a grand house in the latest style. He employed the Dutch architect Balthasar Gerbier to produce designs for it in 1662, but Gerbier died the following year and the work was taken on by William Winde. Completed in 1665 it was a magnificent, even palatial, house, later drawn by the artist William Kip. According to the architectural historian Nicolaus Pevsner;

Kip's drawing (1707) shows a three-storeyed building south of the church arranged round three sides of an

Top: Lord Craven's mansion in Drury Lane, London, and below, his new palace at Hamstead Marshall, after an engraving by Johannes Kip and Leonard Knyff.

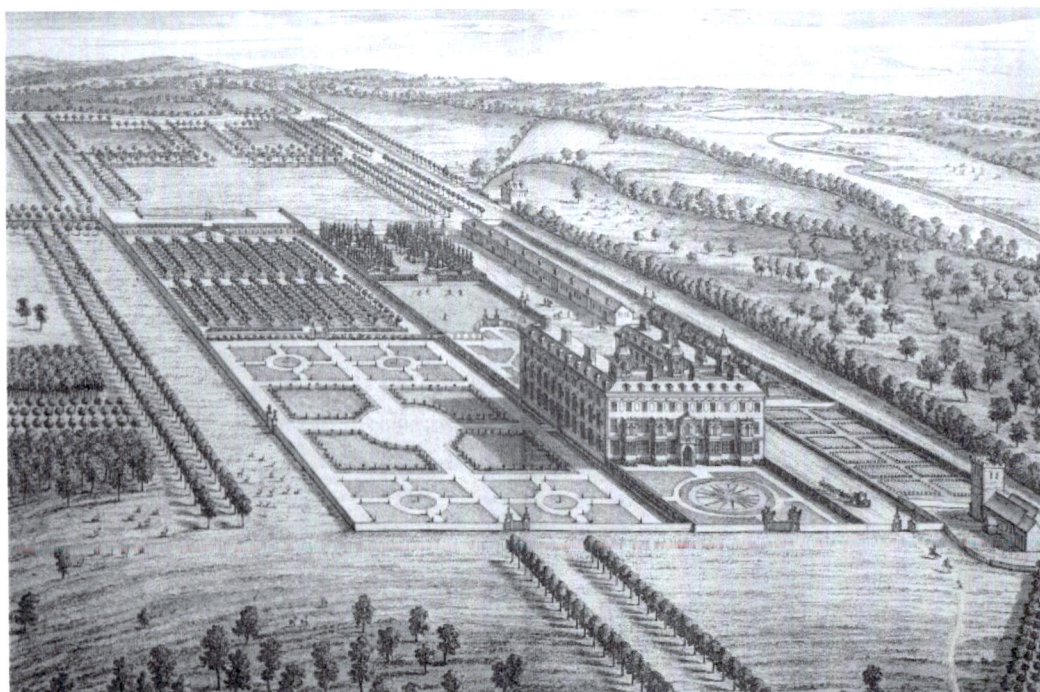

open courtyard, with hipped roofs and three belvedere cupolas and surrounded by formal walled gardens; the detailing may [also] have owed something to the *Palazzi di Genova* .....[10]

In her will Elizabeth repaid some of Craven's lifelong generosity by bequeathing him her magnificent collection of paintings. Like her brother, Charles I, she loved art and while in exile at the Hague she became a patron of the renowned Dutch painter Gerrit van Honthorst (1592-1656). As a talented young man he had trained in Rome where he was deeply influenced by the work of Caravaggio and developed a special skill in 'chiaroscuro' painting, in which his canvases are sometimes lit by a single candle: he was also an extremely gifted portraitist. Elizabeth commissioned many paintings from him and paid him to give drawing lessons to herself as well as to her children, especially Louise, who developed into an able artist. Honthorst painted a huge allegorical portrait of Charles I and Queen Henrietta Maria as Diana and Apollo which is still one of the treasures of Hampton Court and Charles commissioned from him a large painting of Frederick, Elizabeth and their numerous children. He also undertook commissions from the king of Denmark. In addition to Honthorst, Elizabeth was also a great admirer of Rubens, van Dyke, Lely and other fashionable painters of the day.

A catalogue of the Craven collection of paintings compiled in 1866 numbers among the total of 456 works at least 73 by Honthorst, 25 by Sir Anthony van Dyke or his studio, eleven by Lucas Cranach, five by Holbein, four by Caravaggio, four by Mytens, three by Teniers, two by Rembrandt and one by Rubens. Among them are two portraits of Frederick and Elizabeth by Honthorst and one of Charles I by Mytens as well as several portraits by van Dyke of Elizabeth's children Maurice and Rupert and of the Princess of Orange, as well as a portrait of Craven himself, by Honthorst.[11] Most, if not all, of these would have come to Craven through Elizabeth's bequest and many of them were hung initially at Combe Abbey, though some might have been earmarked for Hamstead Marshall and Ashdown when building there was finished.

The completion of Hamstead Marshall in 1665, which then became Craven's main seat, was a momentous year in his career because in recognition of his loyalty to the royalist cause and probably his continued funding of Charles II, in March of that year he was elevated in the peerage as Earl of Craven and Viscount Uffington. His title of Baron Craven had originated from his surname but the earldom very appropriately denoted a large area of North Yorkshire which was, and still is, known as Craven and which includes the birthplace of Sir William Craven, originator of the family fortune. Uffington, with its famous prehistoric 'White Horse' design marked out on a hillside, was chosen because Craven owned the manor of Uffington as well as many estates in the surrounding counties of Oxfordshire and Berkshire. Indeed, Craven's houses at Hamstead Marshall, Benham and Ashdown all lay within a few miles of each other, giving rise to the notion that this was 'Craven country'.

With Craven resident at Hamstead Marshall from 1685, Combe Abbey was leased for £100 a year to Craven's godson and agent Sir Isaac Gibson, who between 1667 and 1669 built a modest new wing on the south west corner of the house. This structure, which still survives, had three gables facing west and made the view of the house from the south look unbalanced. At the same time a very fine seven-light window was constructed on the first floor of the south front.[12]

Meanwhile Craven was showered with many responsibilities. He was given command of an infantry regiment in 1662 and he played a significant part in the City of London's response to the twin disasters of the Plague of 1665 and the Great Fire of 1666, organizing the burial of plague victims and the closure of infected houses as well as directing firefighters while mounted on a handsome white horse that became famous for its bravery. His own London home, Craven House, stood in Drury Lane on the site of a house once owned by the eponymous Sir Robert Drury. It was rebuilt by Craven as a five-storey mansion with eleven small windows on each storey, intersected by Doric and Ionic pilasters. A pair of entrance gates led into a large yard with room for carriages to manoeuvre, and at the back there was a fine garden. According to Edward Brayley, who wrote a topographical history of London in 1829, 'on the wall at the bottom of Craven Buildings there was formerly a fresco painting of the Earl of Craven, who was represented in armour, mounted on a charger, and with a truncheon in his hand. This portrait was twice or thrice repainted in oil, but is now entirely obliterated.' The original fresco is said to have been painted as an expression of gratitude to the earl from London citizens for his hard work as a firefighter but it disappeared after Craven House was demolished in 1809.[13]

After his impressive performance during the Great Fire Craven was promoted lieutenant general in 1667 and in 1670 he was given command of the Coldstream Guards, appointed lord lieutenant of Middlesex and put in charge of the defence of London the following year. In addition to these military duties, Craven was very active in business enterprises. In 1663, as a reward for his loyalty to the Stuarts, he became one of the proprietors of the new colony of 'Carolina' founded in America, where 'Craven County' is still named after him. Two hundred years later his heirs still owned around 700,000 acres of land in Carolina, but it had not been developed and was not even by then particularly valuable.[14] In 1668 Craven was a sponsor, with Prince Rupert and others, of an expedition which set out to find a north-west passage to the Pacific Ocean. By 1670 he was a governor of the Hudson's Bay Company and in 1673 he became a commissioner for Tangier, a major trading post.

When Charles II was faced with a political crisis in 1681 he held a parliament in Oxford for security reasons and Craven was entrusted with command of the military in London, with instructions to repress any attempt at rioting or insurrection. After the death of Charles II in 1685 he continued to be a privy councillor and to hold high military command under his brother James II from 1685 and only surrendered his forces in London to the invading William of Orange in 1688 when instructed to do so by James. Though still vigorous, he was by now eighty years old and the new King William deprived him of his political and military posts, which gave him the opportunity to spend the last years of his life caring for his many houses and gardens.[15]

Craven had no children and of his two younger brothers one died unmarried at eighteen so the remaining brother, John, was for many years his recognized heir. Born in 1610, John studied law at the Middle Temple and in 1634 made a good marriage to Elizabeth, the daughter of Lord Spencer and grand-daughter of the Earl of Southampton. When the civil war began he offered financial support to Charles I and was rewarded with a peerage in his own right as Baron Craven of Ryton. Unfortunately he died childless in 1648 leaving his considerable fortune to members of his family and good causes, including four scholarships of £25 to be awarded at the universities of Oxford and Cambridge. These 'Craven Scholarships', worth rather more these days, are still awarded to classical scholars of distinction.

By the 1680s Craven's recognized heir was his distant cousin Sir William Craven, the great-grandson of his father's brother. Born in 1638 this Sir William married and raised a family and when Craven was created an earl and a viscount in 1665 he was named as heir to the barony of Craven of Hamstead Marshall, though not to the earldom or viscountcy. In 1680 he moved to Combe Abbey to live there with his wife and family. No doubt financed by Lord Craven, ambitious plans were soon made for a complete re-modelling of Lord Harington's Elizabethan house to bring it more into line with the contemporary magnificence of Hamstead Marshall. The decision to rebuild was also prompted by the fact that, as Sir William Craven reported, the timber and walls of the original west wing were extremely rotten and decayed and supported only by several buttresses which prevented the whole structure from collapse. [16]

The architect chosen for the new designs was Lord Craven's godson William Winde, (whose surname rhymes with 'find'). He lived from 1645 to 1722 and he is considered to be one of the most important country house architects of the late seventeenth century. A Dutch gentleman by birth, he had been a soldier in the royalist cause and Craven was his first major patron, employing him at Hamstead Marshall and Caversham Park, after which Winde designed the original Cliveden House and then Buckingham House in London (now encased by the present palace), as well as the fine Belton House in Lincolnshire. His designs for a new west range at Combe were most impressive but the overall impact was ruined by the very regrettable decision to construct only about two-thirds of his scheme, leaving Isaac Gibson's entirely incongruous wing intact.

Winde's new west range, completed in 1684, was two storeys in height and constructed in local grey sandstone with a hipped roof and tall chimneys. On the ground floor there was a 'Great Parlour' with adjoining Drawing Room and kitchens beyond. A finely decorated staircase, carved by Jonathan Wilcox, led to a suite of state apartments on the upper floor, the ceilings decorated with outstanding plasterwork by Edward Gouge and panelling carved by Edward Pierce – all three of these recognized as master craftsmen of their age. There is no doubt that the new west wing was impressive: in 1814 it was noted that 'few ancient mansions contain ranges of apartments better suited to purposes of State and dignified hospitality', while 'Country Life' photographs of 1909 reveal the original decoration of the rooms to be intact and show the walls still lined with the paintings bequeathed by Elizabeth of Bohemia. Other major alterations to the house,

A drawing of the new west range at Combe Abbey, designed by
Lord Craven's godson, William Winde, c 1684. His initial plan
provided for the demolition of the earlier wing (on the right)
built for Sir Isaac Gibson only fifteen years earlier but this
never happened, leaving the west front with contrasting
architectural styles.

undertaken between 1684 and 1689, included the redecoration of the Old Hall with more splendid carving and a new plaster ceiling by Gouge, while a new staircase led to the 'Jacobean great chamber or Dining Room', with a chapel beneath.[17]

Sir William Craven was able to enjoy the amenities of his fine new house for a few years but he never became the second Baron Craven because he died in 1695 at the age of fifty-seven while his magnificent cousin, whom we might call 'The Cavalier Earl' lived on until April 1697, breathing his last at his Drury Lane house in London, aged eighty-nine. It is perhaps significant that he chose to be buried in Binley Parish Church, near Combe Abbey, suggesting that of all his fine residences, Combe meant the most to him. By any standards, he was a very remarkable man and a great survivor – of the battlefield, of the plague, of political upsets, of financial setbacks and of age itself.

It has been suggested by Professor Malcom Smuts that Craven did not reach the very highest levels of political success because he lacked a degree of common sense or had a streak of eccentricity that could unbalance his judgement, while his years of adoring support given to Elizabeth of Bohemia are certainly unusual.[18] On the other hand it is said that 'a fool and his money are easily parted' but this is certainly not the case with Craven. He inherited a vast fortune and spent it liberally, even prodigally, yet while this might have ruined others, it did not ruin him. Quite clearly he employed agents who managed his affairs very ably, even during the difficult years of the interregnum, and he himself became a businessman with international interests so that after 1660 he bounced back in a way so spectacular that his wealth was a major talking point among his contemporaries. He achieved the high distinction of an earldom and left England populated with several fine country houses and gardens – and all without the guiding hand of a wife. How appropriate was the Latin family motto he adopted: 'Virtus in Actione Consistit' – Virtue consists in action.

Chapter Four

The Georgians

Four sporting barons, 1697-1769

The branch of the Craven family who were heirs to the Cavalier Earl descended from his father's brother Henry (1546-1603) who married Margaret Brockden. Henry's surviving son Robert, (1574-1661) who was first cousin to the earl, married Mary Shearwood and his elder surviving son, Sir William Craven of Lenchwick, Worcestershire, made a very advantageous match when he married in 1646 Elizabeth, a daughter of the highly influential Parliamentarian general, Lord Fairfax. Unfortunately they had no children before Sir William Craven died in 1655, so the line of inheritance passed down to his younger brother Thomas (1611-1682), who married Anne Procter. They both hailed from their ancestral North Yorkshire and remained based in Burnsall, where Thomas was buried. Their son Sir William Craven (1638-1695) married Margaret, the daughter of Sir Christopher Clapham of Beamsley, Yorks, and it was he, as the Cavalier Earl's first cousin three times removed, who was named heir to the Craven barony in 1665. In his early married life he lived at Benham Valence, the fine old house and estate near Newbury, Berks. This had been added to the Cavalier Earl's possessions when he was a young man in 1630 and was clearly considered a suitable home for his heir until 1680 when, as we have seen, Sir William moved into Combe Abbey and supervised its rebuilding.

Because Sir William died two years before the earl it was his son, also William – very much a favoured family name – who inherited the barony of Craven of Hamstead Marshall which had been remaindered to his father in 1665. This second Lord Craven was a young man of thirty-one when one of the richest inheritances in the land fell upon his shoulders in April 1697. In October that year he married Elizabeth Skipwith, who came from a gentry family based at Newbold in Warwickshire and together they were able to take stock of their possessions, which included houses and estates at Hamstead Marshall, Combe Abbey, Ashdown House, Benham Valence, Caversham Park and Stokesay Castle, among others.

For reasons that we do not know William decided to sell Caversham Park that same year, though the other properties were retained. A son and heir (also William) was born to the couple in 1700 and a 'spare' who was named Fulwar after his mother's brother, soon followed in 1702. Sadly, after only seven years of marriage, Elizabeth died in childbirth in 1704 and Craven did not marry again. Contemporaries wrote about this time that he 'hath a very good estate, loves field sports and a bottle, [and] is very fat and fair'.[1] He was a governor and 'lord palatine' of Carolina and he served as lord lieutenant of Berkshire and high steward of Newbury but it seems that his main seat was Combe Abbey and the other houses were either leased out or used for occasional visits. In 1702 he commissioned a survey of twenty-six Craven estates which revealed that Hamstead Marshall had twenty-nine tenancies, third in number after Uffington and Stokesay.[2] Despite his great wealth William appears to have been content with his role as a country gentleman and his responsibilities as a lord-lieutenant, which were not inconsiderable. In any case, any further ambitions he may have had were cut short because he died in October 1711 a few days before his forty-third birthday.

This left his elder son, William, to succeed as the third baron but he was only eleven years old and he and his younger brother Fulwar were now orphans placed in the care of their late mother's brother, Sir Fulwar Skipwith.[3] They were soon packed off to school at Rugby, which at this time was essentially still a local grammar school which

William, third baron Craven (1700-1739). He succeeded his
father the second baron (1668-1711), who was the heir, though a
very distant cousin, of the 'Cavalier Earl'. In 1733 he acquired
land in Bayswater, London, on which stand the present streets
named Craven Hill, Craven Hill Gardens and Craven Terrace.
His wife died in childbirth and he left no male heirs.

took in boarders, so that there were about a hundred pupils in all. The Revd Henry Holyoake had been headmaster there since 1688 and it was he who, over a period of forty-three years, very considerably raised the profile of the school so that it was able to attract sons of the local nobility and gentry such as the Cravens: boys of their class at the time would more normally have gone to board at Eton or Westminster, or been tutored at home. Holyoake was a capable scholar and both boys received a good grounding in the classics. Domestically they were in the care of the head's cousin, Judith, whom he described as 'very serviceable and seemingly kind to the boys'. So perhaps their schooldays were reasonably enjoyable. [4]

William went up to St John's College Cambridge in 1716 (aged sixteen) and it was while he was studying there that disaster overcame Hamstead Marshall which was almost totally destroyed by fire. Coal fires in almost every room of a great country house in the winter, fuelled by servants who could be careless, were a constant risk though this particular fire might have been caused by workmen who left a brazier burning untended on the roof. William was devastated because he had become very fond of Hamstead Marshall and had intended to make his home there. He determined to build another house and commissioned the architect James Gibbs to make a start on one, but work ceased after his death.[5] Little now remains of the original great house except for a few ornamental gate-posts, though in due course William did construct a smaller hunting-lodge close by. Combe Abbey therefore remained William's main home, while his brother Fulwar, after completing his studies at Magdalen College, Oxford, took charge of Benham Valence.

In 1721, the year that he reached his majority, William married Anne Tilney of Ritherwick in Hampshire, who brought with her an income of £4,000 a year. Despite his youth, Craven was by now a trustee of Rugby School where a pupil wrote a piece entitled 'the Happy Nuptials' a dialogue in verse between three speakers, performed to celebrate his wedding. A further performance, consisting of a 'Hymn to Diana' celebrated the birth soon afterwards of a daughter, though as the Victorian historian of Rugby remarks, 'in spite of all prayers to various heathen deities, no son came to Lord Craven...'[6]

The Cravens lived together at Combe Abbey for most of the decade until Anne's death in 1729. She was only a young woman but childbirth was full of dangers in this period, as were the dreaded diseases of smallpox and consumption, for which there was no cure. Anne was unable to provide her husband with an heir and he remained unmarried for the rest of his life. In 1733 he acquired nine acres of land in Bayswater, including Upton farm house which he demolished and replaced with a large new house surrounded by ornamental pleasure grounds and ponds. Set well back from the Uxbridge road, it provided him with a convenient home within easy reach of central London. The house and its surrounding fields were passed down to William's successors until 1825 when the Bayswater estate was divided among several members of the family and let on building leases, resulting in the construction of new terraced houses on streets named Craven Hill, Craven Hill Gardens and Craven Terrace, all of which survive today.[7]

Unfortunately, Lord Craven did not have long to enjoy his new London house because he died in 1739 without reaching forty and was buried at Binley. His own experience as an orphan was no doubt behind his support for Thomas Coram's new Foundling Hospital in London, intended 'for the education and maintenance of exposed and deserted young children', but the building in Bloomsbury was not completed until 1745 and although Craven's name appears on the list of founding governors, it is only one among 72 peers and many other influential dignitaries.

William's death without heirs meant that his younger brother Fulwar became the fourth Lord Craven, moving from Benham to occupy Combe Abbey. He was interested in politics and fully intended to stand for election as MP for Berkshire but his brother's death projected him instead into the House of Lords. His main enthusiasm in life was field sports and he was instrumental in founding the Craven Hunt in 1739, centred on the Berkshire Downs and within easy reach of Hamstead Marshall, where he developed the hunting lodge in the Park, and Ashdown and Benham, where he kept his hounds. In addition to hunting Fulwar was very keen on horse racing and maintained his own stud and initiated race meetings on the Lambourn Downs, near Ashdown House.

In 1743 Fulwar was painted by the noted equestrian artist James Seymour in his picture 'A Kill at Ashdown Park', said to be the first depiction of fox-hunting, which remained in the family until 1968 and is now in the collection of Tate Britain. Another painting by Seymour, at present unlocated, is known to show Fulwar hunting the hare (or coursing) with his favourite two greyhounds. Fulwar's estates covered some 70,000 acres over several counties and their affairs, coupled with his sporting life and occasional attendance at court and in the House of Lords, no doubt occupied his time but he never married and in the 1760s it seems that he developed a long and painful illness. This did not prevent him hunting, however, and he was still in the saddle until 1764, the year he died. He chose to be buried in the churchyard at Hamstead Marshall, the first head of the family to be laid to rest there.

With two brothers dying childless, the Craven barony passed to a distant cousin, whose name was nevertheless William. Born in 1705, this fifth Lord Craven was the son of John Craven, a younger brother of the second baron and as a young man, long before he inherited the barony, he became a London property developer. The business-minded Cavalier Earl had bought some ancient 'messuages' near the Strand in 1678 but had left them untouched and they came into the possession of the future fifth baron by inheritance in 1727. Well aware that London was rapidly expanding, he demolished the existing properties and between 1730 and 1735 built 'Craven Street' with twenty fine town

Fulwar Craven (1702-1764), the younger brother of the third baron, succeeded him as the fourth baron and was a keen sportsman who founded the Craven hunt in 1739. He died unmarried and was succeeded by a distant cousin, William, the fifth baron (1705-1769). Portrait by James Latham, courtesy of Miles Barton Period Paintings.

houses on the west side and fifteen on the east side. In the late 1780s his son the sixth baron built another four houses on the west side and six on the east side of the street, which remains to this day a fine example of Georgian architecture in the heart of London and for many years provided a healthy income for its Craven landlords.[8]

In 1746 William Craven was elected MP for Warwickshire and he remained the sitting member for twenty years until he succeeded to the barony. In 1749, rather late in life, he married Rebecca Green, of Coventry, but they had no children. Like his predecessors he was appointed high steward of Newbury, a largely honorary post offered to successive Lords Craven to give a degree of prestige and stability to the town's civic affairs, which were in effect run by an elected mayor and council. William and Rebecca occupied Combe Abbey, but only for five years because he died in March 1769 – though as the dowager Lady Craven Rebecca lived on in another of the family properties until 1791.

Combe and Capability Brown

The barony now passed to the fifth Lord Craven's nephew, yet another William, who was the son of his younger brother the Revd John Craven, who married Mary Hickes and served as Vicar of Staunton Lacy and Rector of Felton in Shropshire until his death in 1752, when he was in his early forties. William, up to then raised in a parson's vicarage, was only fourteen when his father died and responsibility was taken for him by his father's younger brother Thomas, a naval officer who reached the rank of rear-admiral. As befitted the son of a parson who was a graduate of Christ Church at Oxford, William was intellectually able and after school he studied at Balliol successfully enough to be admitted to All Souls, though neither college at this period was the intellectual power house that they later became. Although many noblemen did attend the university during the

William, the sixth Lord Craven (1738-1791) succeeded his uncle the fifth baron and married Lady Elizabeth Berkeley, one of the most beautiful and most intellectual women of her day. Between them they employed 'Capability' Brown to transform the landscape at Combe and also built the small 'Craven Cottage' at Fulham in London.

eighteenth century, wearing a special gown and a black hat with a gold tassel to emphasise their social status, they did not really need to pass the exams for a degree, unlike most undergraduates who had their eye on a career in the church or the law. Joseph Foster's register of Oxford alumni records that Henry, the brother of the fifth baron, as well as the sixth baron and his father actually earned their degrees but the third and fifth barons were granted the honorary higher degree of Doctor of Civil Law (DCL), perhaps in recognition of benefactions to the university or other services rendered.

Maria, a younger sister of the new Lord Craven's father, married Thomas Leigh, the fourth Lord Leigh of Stoneleigh Abbey, which established a family link between the two neighbouring houses of Combe and Stoneleigh but it was not until he was 29, in 1767 that, having no doubt considered several suitable young women as marriage partners, Craven fell deeply in love with Lady Elizabeth Berkeley. Aged only sixteen she was a daughter of the fourth Earl of Berkeley and destined to be not only pretty and charming, but one of the most intellectual of aristocratic women. They married in that year and in her memoirs his wife recalled the early days with her new husband:

> His heart was naturally good; he had received what was called a polished education, though, perhaps, he had not cultivated his mind to the extent that the opportunities which he had might have afforded. His life was one continued ramble: to hunt in Leicestershire, to drive the Oxford stage-coach, to see a new play in London – to visit [his uncle] at Combe Abbey or Admiral Craven at Benham, were his continued occupations. He had a dislike to remain longer than three weeks at a time at any place which when I observed, he kissed my hand and replied – 'Till I lived with you, my love, I never stayed three days in one place'.[9]

Lady Elizabeth Berkeley (1750-1828), the wife of the sixth Lord
Craven, was a writer, playwright, traveller and also a great
admirer of men. She separated from her husband and after his
death she married the Margrave of Anspach and became a
Princess of the Holy Roman Empire.

Chapter Four

In retrospect Elizabeth regretted that despite his intelligence, Craven had 'neither taste for music nor the fine arts. He disliked reading anything but newspapers....' She was also worried that he 'might dissipate his fine fortune' by living beyond his income. When she raised this topic with him on several occasions, he offered to 'give me half his estates and let me be the manager of the whole', a generous offer which she doubtless regretted not taking up after they eventually separated. She might also have mentioned that her husband was a keen member of the recently-founded Jockey Club and a supporter of racing at Newmarket, where the first Craven Meeting took place in 1771, with fourteen competitors. It became an annual fixture and is now a three-day event, culminating in the Craven Stakes.

When his uncle died in 1769 Craven and Elizabeth moved to Combe Abbey, which had been little altered throughout the century, and they decided that it needed to be brought into line with the most fashionable tastes. This was the age of the landscape gardener Lancelot Brown, nicknamed 'Capability' because he used the word often when discussing the potential of a suggested commission. The fifth son of an obscure yeoman farmer from Northumberland he was employed as a gardener when a boy and soon showed that he had an exceptional talent for the imaginative creation of landscape vistas, nearly always involving a lake. He made his name in the 1740s after Lord Cobham appointed him head gardener at Stowe, where he played an important part in the creation of the highly influential garden landscape there. He became 'freelance' in the 1750s and was hugely in demand, earning a fortune for himself. After the accession of George III he was appointed head gardener at St James's, Hampton Court and Richmond and during the 1760s he worked on no less than sixty-five commissions, including Blenheim Palace.[10]

By the 1770s, then, he was very experienced and very expensive but Lord Craven, encouraged by his wife, commissioned him in 1771 to remodel the gardens and park at Combe Abbey. Brown had little time for the formal sixteenth century parterre gardens created by the Cavalier Earl and they disappeared, while the Smite stream was dammed, extensive land was excavated, embankments were built and a ninety-acre lake was created, some six to eight feet deep. On its south side there was the 'deer park', open land planted with oak, ash, beech and some Lebanese cedar trees, while there was more dense woodland to the north. The house was approached by a grand new entrance driveway complete with a triumphal arch in Roman style, while a smaller gothic entrance was provided to the east. At the far end of the lake a 'menagerie' was constructed which may have housed exotic animals or been used as a hunting lodge: it had an octagonal wing with a domed roof which was probably an observatory. To the south of the house were new kennels for the hounds, built in the gothic 'folly' style with fake castle walls and battlements. The park was criss-crossed by carriage drives and the work took six years to complete at a cost itemised in the accounts as £7,650, though Lady Craven later claimed that Brown's bills totalled £12,000. At about this time Lord Craven also rebuilt the parish church at Binley in a light and airy style similar to that of Robert Adam.[11]

As for the house itself, a third storey was added to the courtyard side of the north range, while on the ground floor of the west range a new dining room, eventually called 'the Brown Parlour' was created out of two existing rooms, while several 'Adam' style fireplaces were installed in some of the state rooms. The diarist and routinely critical traveller John Byng visited the house in 1789 but was not impressed by the appearance of the new park and gardens, complaining that Brown had felled too many avenues of trees without replacing them, that the water in the lake was stagnant and that there was 'no inequality of ground'. He thought the main entrance to the house was 'mean', and inside he complained that the cloister passages were too full of trophy antlers and even a stuffed wild cat. However, he was impressed by some of the rooms:

Lancelot 'Capability' Brown (1716-1783) was the most
famous landscape architect of his age, responsible for
hundreds of major projects throughout Britain. He was
commissioned to remodel the grounds at Combe Abbey
in 1771 and subsequently created a ninety-acre lake
surrounded by extensive landscaped parkland.

The old hall, now the dining-room, is a lofty and magnificent apartment, the great dining room at the top of the large staircase is in the same superb style, a kind of room that they will not now build! It is preserved in all state, with sashes, and is a room I should dote upon. The long gallery adjoining is covered by noble portraits of the Cravens, of Gustavus Adolphus and those warriors distinguished in the Palatinate War. The gallery is narrow and low and the pictures have been shamefully cleaned…In the newer part of the house, particularly in the drawing room, are many charming pictures, some by [Murillo] I think. We surveyed every part of the house with pleasure and delay and we were only surprised at the want of a chapel. [The original Harington chapel had been removed in the Winde scheme.][12]

While work was under way at Combe Abbey, a fire disaster struck again at a Craven estate when the house at Benham Valence went up in flames in 1773. William and Elizabeth saw this as an opportunity to build themselves a brand new house in the latest fashion and commissioned Henry Holland to design a classical gem. Lancelot Brown was consulted over the gardens but Elizabeth vowed that she would do most of the design herself because of the prices he charged. The new house was ready by 1775 and the couple, thrilled with their modern creation, tended to stay there more often than the rather outdated Combe Abbey.

During the 1770s Elizabeth was very fully occupied. Her first daughter, Maria, was born in 1769 and her first son, William, in the following year, while four other children followed steadily. She managed to spend a good deal of time in London where she enjoyed the company of intellectuals such as Dr Johnson and his faithful

A watercolour of Combe Abbey painted c.1810.
The perspective is not quite right in this view
of the south front as it was then.

Boswell, who described her as 'the beautiful, gay and fascinating Lady Craven'. She was also a friend of Horace Walpole who helped to develop her literary talent: she wrote translations and short stories as well as a number of plays, fables, pantomimes and light farces which were performed at Benham 'for the benefit of the local poor', though they were not very successful in London theatres.[13]

Unfortunately for her reputation Elizabeth could not resist the charms of other men and had a well-publicised affair in 1773 with the French ambassador, the Duc de Guines, followed by a number of other scandalous liaisons. This led her husband to take mistresses, so the family atmosphere at Combe Abbey and Benham must often have been strained. In 1780, perhaps to please a whim of Elizabeth, Craven built a small house on a piece of his land close to the River Thames near Putney. The foundations of this 'Craven Cottage', which burnt down in 1888, lie beneath the central circle on the pitch of the present Fulham Football Ground, established there six years later and named after it.

In 1783 matters came to a head, the couple separated and Lord Craven gave Elizabeth an income of £1,500 a year. Taking only one of her children with her, the four-year-old Keppel, she lived close to Versailles, wrote pieces for the French court and met Frederick, sovereign prince (or 'Margrave') of Anspach, in northern Germany, with whom she developed a close friendship, despite the fact that he was a married man. Horace Walpole met her in Paris late in 1785 and wrote 'she is very pretty, has parts [talent], and is good-natured to the greatest degree, has not a grain of malice or mischief ...and has never been an enemy but to herself'.[14] Between 1783 and 1786 Elizabeth travelled to many countries in Europe and the near East in the company of Frederick and in 1789 she published 'A Journey through the Crimea to Constantinople', her most significant work.

Meanwhile Lord Craven contented himself with his own mistress, Mrs Byrne, with whom he lived happily and he proved to be a conscientious manager of his many estates, commissioning detailed reviews of his tenants and the dues they owed. Although he attended the House of Lords from time to time he was famous for not contributing a word to the debates until, according to his wife, writing to a friend, he got to his feet after a speech from a government minister and uttered the immortal words 'That is a lie', and sat down again without further comment, to widespread laughter from their lordships.[15] During the course of 1791 he fell victim to a terminal illness and died in September while on a visit to Lausanne.

The earldom recreated, 1791-1825

Craven's death led to a flurry of events. First of all his eldest son William, aged twenty-one, succeeded him as the seventh baron and very soon afterwards his widow married Frederick of Anspach (whose ailing wife had died earlier in the year) in a glittering ceremony in Lisbon, where the bride was radiant in a white satin gown, heavily laden with diamonds. The margrave, who had no male heir, sold his principality to his cousin the King of Prussia for a fine sum in 1790 and he and Elizabeth soon moved to Brandenburg House, an impressive mansion by the Thames at Fulham which boasted its own theatre and there they entertained on a lavish scale. Francis II, the Holy Roman Emperor, granted Elizabeth the title of Princess in 1793 but George III and the English court refused to recognize it and still regarded her as a loose woman.

Meanwhile her eldest son William, a very dashing fellow, was pursuing a military career with considerable success. He went to school at Eton, joined the Berkshire militia at the age of fifteen and in 1793, when republican France declared war on Britain after guillotining its king, Craven spent a small fortune on buying a commission as lieutenant colonel of the 84th Regiment of Foot, said to be the largest amount ever paid for that rank. He then fought under the command of the Duke of York, George III's second and favourite son, in the Flanders campaigns of 1793-5, when York's relatively small English army worked together with Austrian and German allies in an unsuccessful attempt to defeat the forces of the new French republic. After this Craven served under General Abercromby in the West Indies, where islands such as Grenada, St Vincent and Trinidad were wrested from Spanish control. No doubt recommended by the Duke of York, who was by then Commander-in-Chief of the British Army, Craven was promoted colonel and appointed an ADC to the king in 1798 and served with York's troops in a short campaign in North Holland in 1799. Clearly he was an able officer and he won the respect of the Duke of York and King George for his professional abilities and seems to have been liked by Queen Charlotte, possibly because of his undoubted good looks and charm.

About this time Craven sold the splendid house and estate at Benham Park to his mother and her husband for use as a country home in addition to Brandenburg House in London. They lived there on a grand scale until the margrave died in 1806, leaving Elizabeth £150,000. She subsequently travelled a good deal abroad and in 1819 settled in Naples, building the 'Villa Craven' near Posilipo. She died there in 1828, leaving the villa and Benham Park to her bachelor youngest son Keppel. In 1848 he sold Benham on, so it ceased to be part of the Craven family estate.

In June 1801 George III, no doubt after consultation with his prime minister, Henry Addington, took the unusual step of recreating the earldom of Craven and the viscountcy of Uffington and bestowing both titles on his ADC, still only a young colonel, who thereby became the first Earl of Craven of the second creation. Given that both the king and his wife regarded Craven's mother as not a fit person to be received at court, his elevation in the peerage is surprising, even though he was respected and liked by the royal couple. But the years from 1800

William, the dashing seventh baron and first Earl of Craven of the second creation, (1770-1825). His great wealth and opposition to Catholic Emancipation resulted in his elevation to the earldom at a comparatively young age in 1801, several years before his controversial marriage to an actress. He was a successful soldier and keen yachtsman but left huge debts to his heir. He built the 'royal tennis' court at Combe. Portrait by Sir Thomas Lawrence, courtesy of the National Army Museum.

to 1801 were very difficult ones for George III: by the end of 1800 all Britain's allies against France had been defeated and there was serious unrest in Ireland, which led to the decision to pass the Act of Union early in 1801, creating the United Kingdom of Great Britain and Ireland. Moreover, George's trusted prime minister, William Pitt the Younger, was determined to repeal the laws restricting the freedom of Catholics: but the king would not allow this because he believed it to be contrary to promises made in his coronation oath. This resulted in Pitt's regretful resignation in February 1801, a major blow for the king.

These anxieties contributed to a bout of mental illness suffered by George III between February and March, which delayed the appointment of Pitt's successor, Henry Addington, whose somewhat shaky administration was in place by the end of March. Craven's earldom was formalized in June and it is very likely that it was a reward not so much for his relatively routine military service or his personal loyalty to the king and queen as an ADC during this difficult period, but for his political support in the House of Lords for the Act of Union, for his backing of Addington in his takeover of office from Pitt and above all for his determined opposition to Catholic Emancipation, to which, like the king, Craven strongly objected. It is also possible that he made a handsome donation to 'national funds'.

The new earl was thirty years old and still unmarried, despite his long-established reputation as a ladies' man. But about this time he caught sight of Harriette Wilson, aged fifteen, the strikingly attractive daughter of a Swiss clockmaker who had a shop in Mayfair. It seems that he persuaded her to leave home and live with him and in 1825, shortly after his death, Harriette described their time together in her published memoirs. She wrote:

> I shall not say why and how I became, at the age of
> fifteen, the mistress of the Earl of Craven. Whether it
> was love, or the severity of my father, the depravity of

my own heart, or the winning arts of the noble lord which induced me to leave my paternal roof and place myself under his protection, does not now much signify; or, if it does, I am not in the humour to gratify curiosity in this matter. I resided on the Marine Parade at Brighton and I remember that Lord Craven used to draw cocoa trees, and his fellows [soldiers] as he called them, on the best vellum paper for my amusement. 'Here stood the enemy', he would say, 'and here, my love, are my fellows. There the cocoa trees, etc.' It was, in fact, a dead bore. All these cocoa trees and fellows, at past eleven o'clock at night, could have no particular interest for a child like myself, so lately in the habit of retiring early to rest. One night, I recollect, I fell asleep and as I often dream I said, yawning and half-awake, 'O Lord! O Lord! Craven has got me into the West Indies again'. In short I soon found that I had made but a bad speculation by going from my father to Lord Craven. I was even more afraid of the latter than I had been of the former. Not that there was any particular harm in the man beyond his cocoa trees; but we never suited or understood each other.

Harriette complained that she was also bored with Craven's enthusiasm for sailing and that he wore an ugly cotton night-cap, and that he never once made her laugh or did anything to please her, and that she eventually tired of all his money and his flashy carriage. Yet she felt she had to remain faithful to him despite being pursued ardently by Frederick Lamb, the very handsome, six-foot son of Lord Melbourne. Aware of the debauched reputation of the Prince of Wales, she decided to try her luck with him: 'I am told that I am very beautiful, so perhaps you would like to see me...', she wrote. One of the prince's friends replied that if she came up to London, she might well be favoured with an 'interview'. Craven employed a black footman called John, whom Harriette supposed 'he had imported with his cocoa-trees from the West Indies', and she decided to post the letter herself in case John should become suspicious. Her second letter to the Prince of Wales began:

> Sir: To travel fifty-two miles this bad weather, merely to see a man, with only the given number of legs, arms, fingers, etc, would, you must admit, be madness in a girl like myself, surrounded by humble admirers who are ever ready to travel any distance for the honour of kissing the tip of her little finger…..

In the end, although she resisted (so she claimed) the advances of Frederick Lamb, someone told Craven that they had often been seen together in Brighton while he was away, and he decided to end the relationship. He told her: 'Let me add, Harriette, that you might have done anything with me, with only a little mere conduct. As it is, allow me to wish you happy, and further, pray inform me if in any way [from a distance] I can promote your welfare.' Sentiments worthy indeed of an officer and a gentleman or a character out of one of Jane Austen's novels.[16]

Fifteen was not an unacceptable age for an affair between a girl and an unmarried man at this time and members of the aristocracy routinely took mistresses. Indeed, as Craven hinted, he might well have married Harriette had she behaved herself, and one of Harriette's sisters did marry a peer. She, however, pursued with notable success a lifetime's career as a courtesan, moving on to Frederick Lamb and then the Duke of Argyll and ultimately many of the beaus of regency England. Indeed, it is said that it was her affair with the Duke of Wellington which led him famously to tell her literary agent, when threatened with exposure, that she could 'publish and be damned'.

The end of Craven's affair with Harriette Wilson did not lead to a permanent relationship with anyone else for the time being and he continued to pursue his military duties energetically. In 1803 he was appointed colonel of the newly-formed ninth battalion of reserves which recruited from Warwickshire among other counties, then after it merged with another battalion in 1805 he was promoted major-general. He ceased to be an ADC to the king in that year and was appointed to the general staff of the army. In 1807 Craven entertained the Prince of Wales for one night at Combe Abbey while the prince was touring Warwickshire and towards the end of the year he at last decided to marry, though his choice did not fall on some suitable lady of the aristocratic class, or even the daughter of a rich merchant who would have bolstered his finances. She was Louisa Brunton, aged twenty-two, the daughter of a Norwich grocer turned actor-manager, and she was well known on the stage at Covent Garden and elsewhere in London as a comedy actress. There was no society wedding, only a quiet ceremony held by special licence in London in December and it cannot be thought that the marriage would have been approved by the court, or indeed by William's mother. The new countess gave up the stage and devoted her life to making her husband happy and providing him with three boys and a girl. They lived at Combe, Ashdown and also in the park at Hamstead Marshall, not far from the site of the old mansion, where they developed 'Hamstead Lodge' into an attractive modern house in the Regency style.

In addition to its magnificent picture collection, Combe Abbey at this time also housed the Craven collection of armour, put together originally in the seventeenth century by the Cavalier Earl and considered to be one of the most impressive in Europe. In addition there were some superb seventeenth-century tapestries from France, Holland and Germany as well as very fine furniture in the

Louisa Brunton, the London comedy actress who married the first Earl in 1807. Despite society eyebrows being raised at this union, the marriage was a happy one.

contemporary taste by Chippendale and Sheraton. Craven made few changes to the house, though he redecorated the cloister walks and in 1803 put an elaborate papier-maché ceiling and Gothic traceried window into a room in the east wing. His main contribution was the construction close to the house of an indoor 'real' (i.e.royal) tennis court sometime after 1810. This ancient 'game of kings', played with a hard ball which could be hit against all four walls was more like modern racquets than its Victorian offshoot, lawn tennis.[17]

Craven was a considerable sportsman, enjoying hunting as well as horse racing, which he developed at Enborne Heath, near Newbury. From early youth he became devoted to sailing and spent a lot of money on a succession of yachts which were by no means modest sailing boats. By 1809 he owned a 285-ton sloop named 'Grafton' which he sailed, lightly armed, in the Channel despite the danger of French privateers. In 1815, after the end of the Napoleonic War, the Royal Yacht Squadron was founded at Cowes and he was one of the original members with his full-rigged three-masted yacht, named 'Louisa' after his wife – of some 325 tons and 150 feet in length. Just before he died he became the proud owner of an even bigger vessel, 'The Mayfly'.[18]

His service over the years in the army was clearly approved by the Commander-in-Chief, Prince Frederick, Duke of York, because he was promoted lieutenant-general in 1811. As well as being high steward of Newbury and a trustee of Rugby School he also served as recorder of Coventry from 1811 to 1825 and as lord lieutenant of Berkshire from 1819 to 1825. In 1825 his army service was recognized by his promotion to full general.[19] Late in the twentieth century it was luridly rumoured, without any evidence, that he might have sired a child by a gypsy girl, who, when rejected, put a curse upon him and his successors. It happens to be the case that he and seven subsequent earls of Craven all died comparatively young - before they were 58 - which is fairly remarkable until it is remembered that of Craven's predecessors, one died at 33, another at 39, one aged 53 and two in their early sixties. The 'curse of the Cravens' as it was described in the tabloids of the 1980s had more to do with gossip than authentic history but, as will be seen, some of the earls of Craven did die young and in quick succession, with calamitous repercussions for the family and its possessions in the twentieth century.

Very soon after his promotion to full general, Craven took lodgings in Cowes where he hoped to convalesce in the fresh air from acute attacks of rheumatic gout, which had troubled him for some time. Unfortunately, complications set in and he died at Cowes on 30 July 1825, aged 54.[20] There can be no doubt that he was an effective soldier and military administrator and it is very likely that he used political influence and some of his wealth in acquiring his earldom. His choice of wife would have given rise to whispers in Society but the couple were happy together and raised a healthy family. He diminished the Craven estate by selling Benham to his mother and ran up very considerable debts as a result of extravagant living, especially the maintenance of large private yachts. In fact he left debts of £273,000, a huge responsibility to fall on the shoulders of his sixteen-year old heir.[21]

Chapter Five

The Victorians

The photographer earl, 1825-1866

William, the second Earl of Craven, was born in July 1809, raised largely at Combe Abbey and sent to school at Eton, where one of the assistant masters was Edward Craven Hawtrey, a distant relative and later headmaster of the school. Craven was still at his studies when his father died so his mother was probably his main guardian as he left school and proceeded to Oxford's grandest college, Christ Church, where he lived in considerable style as a nobleman undergraduate. After university he spent eighteen months from 1829 to 1830 travelling on the continent with a suitable retinue. This was just after the death of his grandmother in 1828 and he was no doubt influenced by her own distinguished career as a traveller to unconventional places. He did not limit his itinerary to the classical 'grand tour' of Italy but also ventured to some of the German principalities as well as Russia and Eastern Europe: given that his grandmother had been a Princess of the Holy Roman Empire it is likely that he was well received in aristocratic and courtly circles. After his safe arrival home he was treated to a reception by the mayor of Coventry and civic dignitaries who presented him with an illuminated address dated 19 October 1830 which read:

> We the Mayor Bayliffs and Commonalty of the City of Coventry in Council Assembled most respectfully beg leave to offer to Your Lordship our warmest congratulations on the return of Your Lordship from

the Continent to Combe Abbey the venerable seat of
Your Lordship's noble Ancestors.[1]

Despite these eminently respectful sentiments, Craven soon
had an unpleasant reminder that the England of 1830 was a restless
nation where few respected the monarchy of George IV and many
resented the widespread enclosure of agricultural land and the
development of new machinery which put labourers out of work.
Moreover, there was a bad harvest that year and many starved. While
Craven was staying with his mother at Hamstead Marshall rioters
destroyed machinery in the nearby village of Kintbury and demanded
money with menaces from landowners. Even Craven himself had to
pay ten pounds to persuade the mob to move on. In due course some
three hundred special constables were recruited from the locality to
search out the culprits and Craven, though not a trained military man,
played a leading role in assisting the Grenadier Guards to restore order:
one offender was hanged and dozens more were transported to the
penal colony in Australia.

A portrait of Craven painted in 1831 by Sir George Hayter
shows him to be slim, dark-haired and the inheritor of the good looks
of both his mother and his father. According to Noel Chanan, whose
recent study of Craven the photographer has revealed much about him
that was not widely known before, the young earl had:

> ....required himself to be portrayed as a fashionably
> Byronic figure, a Romantic, a rebel against conformity.
> He is dressed in appropriate uniform for the part,
> voluminous black cloak drawn casually over an open-
> necked, broad-collared shirt and a clashing red coat; he
> had long, wind-blown hair, and whiskers meeting under
> his chin to form a youthful beard.[2]

William, second Earl of Craven (1809-1866) by Sir George Hayter. He married Lady Emily Grimston, a very well-connected aristocrat and developed an interest in photography. From 1851 onwards he employed William Eden Nesfield to demolish the Tudor east wing at Combe Abbey and reconstruct it in 'Victorian Gothic' style. (NPG).

This was not a young man destined to follow his father in a military career, an unquestioning Tory, like most of his ancestors. He did enjoy hunting and became a keen and successful owner of race horses, but he was also interested in art and architecture and all the latest technological developments: this is probably what prompted him to buy an apartment in Paris in the fashionable Rue de la Paix while still in his early twenties. Soon afterwards his eye was caught by Lady Emily Mary Grimston, aged twenty, a very well-connected young aristocrat. Her father was the Earl of Verulam and her mother the daughter of the first Earl of Liverpool and the half-sister of the second earl, who was prime minister from 1812 to 1827. Moreover Mary's sister Katherine was the wife of the fourth Earl of Clarendon, a highly influential Liberal politician who would be three times foreign secretary and also lord lieutenant of Ireland.

Not that his wife's connections drew Craven into the world of politics. Though a declared Whig and liberally minded, he was not particularly active in Parliament: his wife wrote on one occasion 'I am afraid Craven's devotion to his duties in the House of Lords will not take him to London again today. He has been out hunting this morning.' In the opinion of a family member, he was not a scholar and no great intellectual, but a 'fine horseman and very good to hounds, a first rate all round shot and an extraordinarily fine fly fisherman.' 'A man of ideas and impatient of the common groove', he was 'practical, quick of mind and took a pride in the exercise of manual dexterity, in which he excelled'. He was also an accomplished craftsman and made candlesticks, boxes and other small items, some of which are still owned by members of his family.[3] Craven's new wife was bright and inquisitive and kept diaries full of descriptions of the places they visited and the people they met. She accompanied her husband to Switzerland in 1837 and noted that he romantically presented her with alpine flowers near the famous Reichenbach Falls.

Benham Park was at this time the property of Craven's uncle

Keppel, while his mother lived at Hamstead Lodge. Therefore the two main country houses available to the newly-married Cravens were Combe Abbey and Ashdown and of the two they spent more of their time at Ashdown, perhaps because it was only a few miles away from Louisa at Hamstead and also because it was in the centre of hunting and racing country. It was also less rambling and more manageable. All the same, Combe was an important part of their lives and its six thousand acre estate, which included a stretch of the Oxford canal and a small colliery at Wyken, was a vital source of revenue when added to the twenty thousand acres of family land in Berkshire's 'Craven Country', with another few thousand at Stokesay in Shropshire and elsewhere. Given the enormous debts which he inherited, Craven understood the need to be practical and was successful in reducing his expenses, helped by the fact that agricultural land produced healthy profits for a few decades in the first half of the century, thanks to the infamous 'Corn Laws' which prohibited the import of cheap foreign wheat until the home product reached a very high price – which many poor people could not afford.

In 1839 a Scottish nobleman, the Earl of Eglinton, fired by the romantic historical novels of Sir Walter Scott and a fear that the parliamentary Reform Bill passed in 1832 spelt doom for the traditional English aristocracy, spent a fortune in holding an elaborate medieval-style tournament at Eglinton Castle in Scotland. Only aristocrats were invited to take part and Craven, a contemporary of Eglinton at Eton, was among them, while representing the chivalry of France was the exiled young Prince Louis Napoleon. This was not intended to be a 'mock' event: real jousting took place and original historic armour was used as well as original weapons. Months of preparation and training were undertaken as young noblemen struggled to come to terms with the physical fitness and technical skills required to charge at each other on horseback with heavy lances in the lists.

The tournament was planned for two days, starting on

The second Earl of Craven and his entourage appearing at
the Eglinton tournament in medieval armour as the
'Knight of the Griffin'. Detail from a drawing by J.H. Nixon.

Wednesday 28 August and it drew a crowd of some 60,000 people, while the combatants were accommodated either in the castle or in tented pavilions. Craven appeared as 'the Knight of the Griffin', one of his family's heraldic devices, and he wore a sixteenth century suit of armour, no doubt chosen from his ancestral collection. Both in the practices and in the lists themselves he performed well, winning all his jousts. Unfortunately the entire event was ruined by exceptionally bad weather: the rain sluiced down mercilessly soon after proceedings on the first day so that the colourful finery of the knights and esquires became muddied and bedraggled. It continued to rain until the following afternoon so Lord Eglinton announced that there would be an extension and on Friday the sun shone and the tournament resumed but on Saturday the rain came again and the event had to be abandoned. By then most of the crowds had long gone home, disillusioned. At least no-one was killed or seriously injured, something that frequently happened at tournaments in Plantagenet England.[4]

In tune with the current enthusiasm for the 'Gothic Revival' the Cravens thought seriously in the early 1840s about rebuilding Combe Abbey, possibly in a mock-medieval style. They enjoyed living at Ashdown House but it was technically only a large hunting lodge and lacked the status of their official ancestral seat at Combe. As early as 1834 they had consulted one of the pioneers of the 'Gothic Revival', the architect Lewis Nockalls Cottingham, about alterations to Combe but without any result. Eight years later they approached Edward Blore, a friend of Sir Walter Scott and an admirer of the 'Scottish baronial' style who had worked on restoration projects in many English cathedrals and designed a Gothic palace in Russia as well as the medieval-looking Government House in Sydney, Australia. Blore could also produce more restrained designs and had recently added a well-mannered third storey to 'The Grove', the country seat near Watford of Emily Mary's sister, the Countess of Clarendon. On St Valentine's Day 1842 Emily Mary wrote to Blore:

Ever since the Earl and I have seen the wonders that you have produced at the Grove, we have been most anxious to have the benefit of your opinion about this old house which we are extremely anxious to make more convenient and if possible less expensive for at present it is so straggling a building that without having much available room we find the keeping it in proper repair as more than we can....afford. Would you have the kindness to attempt helping us and do you think you [would] be able to pay us a visit any time before the end of the month.[5]

It seems that Blore did meet the Cravens and that plans were discussed, but unfortunately we do not know what they were. Given the tone of the letter, it is possible that the expense was considered too great. At all events no major architectural change was made to Combe Abbey for another twenty years, although it was maintained in good repair. Craven's interest in technical developments resulted in important innovations at Combe during the early years of his ownership: running water was provided by a gravity feed system which reached all parts of the house from a new reservoir built near the east gate, while a new plant sited half a mile to the north-west of the house produced gas from coal to light the interiors.[6]

For most of the 1840s the Cravens divided their time between Combe and Ashdown, with regular visits to the dowager Countess Louisa at Hamstead Lodge. She was very popular in the locality for her generosity and 'common touch' and she remained on the best of terms with her son and his wife. Craven himself spent most of his time on affairs relevant to his estates or engaged in country pursuits which included riding with the Atherstone Hunt, recently formed and extending over parts of Warwickshire and two adjoining counties. He also enjoyed shooting pheasant at Ashdown and grouse on the Yorkshire moors and stalking deer in Scotland. Meanwhile, his wife bore him a succession of children. Their first baby, Elizabeth, was born in 1836, their son and heir, William, in 1838, Evelyn in 1839, George in 1841, Blanche in 1842, Beatrix in 1844, Emily in 1846, Osbert in 1848 and Robert in 1850.

The National Census of 1851 recorded that the residents of Combe Abbey that year were the earl and countess and seven of their children plus two other family members, two governesses and thirty-three servants. Resident on the estate were a head gardener and ten garden labourers, a coachman, two park keepers, two game keepers and five other employees.[7]

During the 1850s Craven became increasingly fascinated by photography, an interest that may well have been aroused by the London Great Exhibition of 1851 which, among its wonders, displayed some 800 photographic images. The idea of a lensed 'camera' which could reflect images had long been known but a Frenchman, Daguerre, transferred camera images onto a highly-polished plate with a silver surface treated with iodine and then 'developed' the resulting faint image with mercury fumes. This image could be made permanent by using a strong solution of salt to remove the other chemicals. This revolutionary discovery was made known to a meeting of the French Academy of Sciences in January 1839 and having arranged suitable patents Daguerre released details of his 'daguerrotype' process in August and it was greeted with great enthusiasm.

Working quite separately from Daguerre, Henry Fox Talbot, an English landowner in the West Country, managed to transfer stable photographic negatives to paper as early as 1835. In 1841 he patented a process known as 'calotype' by which paper was coated with silver iodide before being exposed to the camera and developed into a translucent negative which could be used to produce multiple copies, unlike a daguerreotype. Fundamentally, this remained the basis of photography until the arrival of digital technology, though Talbot's

Lord Craven's photograph of his Derby winner
'Wild Dayrell' with a groom and two stable-lads
in the grounds of Ashdown House.

calotype was improved by the 'wet collodion' method invented by Frederick Scott Archer, in which the negative was made on a sheet of glass, sharper than paper and requiring less exposure time. Craven worked hard on the calotype process, which involved a good deal of patience and technical skill on his part. His earliest surviving attempts were images of his own portrait as a young man by Hayter, a self-portrait and an image of Archer, which suggests that the inventor may have given Craven personal instruction in the early years. Craven contributed some undistinguished items, including a still life and an image of Ashdown House, to a photographic exhibition held at the Society of Arts in London in 1852 and he eventually joined the Royal Photographic Society which was founded the next year.

Craven was now in his early forties and seemingly fit and active so it must have been a complete shock when on Thursday, 7 September 1854 he suffered a stroke at Ashdown House which paralysed one side of his body as well as affecting his speech and the muscles in his face.[8] There was anxiety in case something more serious developed but after six weeks he recovered sufficiently to return to a fairly normal lifestyle, though he had to curtail his more vigorous country pursuits. In these circumstances his interest in photography became more intense and he acquired a mobile camera and darkroom specially constructed for him by Hooper's the coachbuilders as well as a large camera for glass negatives which was mounted on the chassis of a curricle, a one-horse carriage. Using these contraptions he was able to travel about his estates, especially at Ashdown, making photographic images. This is how he produced his most striking images so far - of his champion racehorse, 'Wild Dayrell'.

Bred by Francis Popham of Littlecote House in Wiltshire, Wild Dayrell was born in 1852 and named rather wickedly after one of Popham's ancestors who was alleged to have thrown his illegitimate baby into a fire at the house, which he had been condemned to haunt ever since. As a colt Wild Dayrell was sold for a hundred guineas to a son of the Duke of Richmond and trained at Goodwood House but showed little early promise and Popham bought him back for 250 guineas. At this point Craven was persuaded to buy a half-share in the stallion, which was by now a strong and impressive brown horse some sixteen hands high and he moved it to Ashdown House where it was trained by Popham's groom, Rickaby and his sons, who were employed as stable boys by Craven.

In September 1854, as a two-year-old, Wild Dayrell so easily won his first race, a three-horse sweepstake at Newmarket, that offers began to be made for him - £3,000 from the Rothschilds, for instance. As a precursor to the 1855 Derby, a private race was arranged against strong competitors to test the horse's ability and he won this easily, which again ramped up his credibility in the eyes of the betting fraternity – so much so that Popham and Craven were offered £5,000 not to enter him for the race. They rejected this and Wild Dayrell started as even money favourite in a field of twelve at Epsom on 27 May 1855. Making his final challenge a furlong from the finish he won by a length, netting much profit for his backers, including a reported £10,000 for Craven. Unfortunately the horse went lame after this race and missed the meeting at Goodwood, though he was entered for the 'Ebor St Leger' at York in August, winning in fine style. His lameness returned in the Doncaster Cup, where he was forced to pull up and this proved to be his last race.

After this short but distinguished career Wild Dayrell was put to stud at Littlecote, where he sired a number of future winners including the champion stallion 'Buccaneer' and he died at Littlecote in 1879. Thanks to his part-owner, Wild Dayrell also has the distinction of being the first winner of the Derby to be photographed. Craven produced two images, one of the horse with Rickaby and his two sons standing in front of Ashdown House and this was exhibited at the Photographic Society of Scotland in 1856. He then created a variant of this image by using opaque liquid on the negative to blank out the house and surrounding trees so that the result was more reminiscent of an animal painting by Stubbs.[9]

One of Craven's favourite photographic subjects was his children and probably his finest image of them was a 'roundel' which portrays all nine sitting on the steps of an entrance to the house at Ashdown. For Noel Chanan, who claims a high place for Craven as a photographer, the many images of his children reveal that Craven was closer to his family than many Victorian fathers:

> Craven's images of his children speak of his intimacy with them, his concern with their development as individuals, as well as speaking eloquently of his own character, where there is no other testimony. The images are evidence of the warmth and tenderness of his love for them, of his gentleness towards them and of his proximity to them. Without the mutual affection of which these sweet images are the expression, they would never have succeeded in their being.[10]

Craven took nearly all his photographs at Ashdown and in addition to his children and Wild Dayrell his subjects were the house itself, trees on the estate, and the parterre garden which was created during the 1850s. In Craven's many images of trees Chanan sees the influence of the German painter Caspar David Friedrich, whose work Craven might well have admired on his tour of northern Europe as a young man. As for the parterre garden, this was designed by the landscape architect William Andrews Nesfield in the early 1850s. He favoured an Italian style which resulted in the new garden at Ashdown being:

> composed of intricate patterns of coloured gravels made from the likes of crushed yellow and red brick and blue Welsh slate laid within borders of dwarf box and beds

of miniature shrubs and incorporating fragments of coloured glass. The style was meant to replicate the ribbon parterre seen in the marble floors of many medieval Italian churches, abstract patterns of a kind that probably originated in Rome in the Middle Ages, where scattered shards and the fragments of stone buildings of antiquity were in plentiful supply and came to be used for decorative flooring.[11]

In the opinion of Noel Chanan, some of Craven's photographs of these parterre gardens are his masterpieces.

During the course of 1856 Craven's relationship with his younger brother, Frederick, became very strained. They had a sister, Louisa, who had married Sir George Johnstone Bt in 1840, but he fell from his horse in the hunting field the next year and was killed. Shortly afterwards his wife gave birth to twin boys and in 1844 she re-married. The boys were heirs to Johnstone land in the United States so their Craven uncles William and Frederick were appointed their trustees and initiated a policy of selling the land through agents in the UK and the USA. In due course Frederick became unhappy with the efficiency of this process and accused his brother of insufficient scrutiny of the agents and their lawyers, who he thought were pocketing too much of the proceeds. The brothers took their dispute to court, though no clear resolution was reached.

The strain of this argument may have contributed to a second stroke suffered by Craven, probably in 1857, the year he resigned the lord-lieutenancy of Warwickshire, which he had held since 1853, on grounds of ill health. All the same he was well enough in November 1858 to accept an invitation from the Emperor Napoleon III, with whom he had been on friendly terms since they had met at the Eglinton Tournament, to join an exclusive party in the forest of Compiègne, near Paris, for a week's hunting and festivities. Also invited were Lord

Palmerston and the Earl of Clarendon, who had until recently been respectively the Whig prime minister and foreign secretary. At a time when the rising power of Napoleon's France was much suspected by the Tory party in the UK, this visit attracted political criticism, even though it was only a private social event. More of a shock for Craven was that his wife received very flattering attention from the Emperor, despite the presence of Napoleon's wife and mistress. Clarendon later wrote of his sister-in-law: 'Lady Mary Craven was immensely admired. The Empress and Madame Walewska were loud in their admiration of her, but towards the end of the week they had very much cooled'. It seems that Napoleon asked the Cravens to stay on, but William made his apologies, and they left for home. A few months later, his much-loved mother Louisa died at home in Hamstead Lodge.[12]

In July 1861 the Cravens departed on an ambitious tour of Europe, taking with them their daughter Evelyn Mary, who was becoming a promising photographer herself. They travelled first to Germany and then through Switzerland to Italy, sailing from Genoa and visiting Elba, Sicily and Naples before reaching Rome in time for Christmas. In the New Year they travelled on to Paris and were back home by the spring of 1862 – a long holiday by any standard. Evelyn Mary celebrated her return by marrying soon enough a son of the Marquess of Ailesbury.

Combe and Victorian Gothic

Now that Ashdown House was fully modernised, both inside and out, the Cravens turned their attention to the needs of Combe Abbey. They had considered making big changes at the house in the 1830s and the 1840s, but nothing had been done and by the early 1860s, when scientific and technological discoveries were being made on a regular basis and when new fashions had been highlighted by the Great

Top: an architect's drawing for a new wing at Combe Abbey and
(below) a photograph of the finished product.

Exhibition in 1851 they decided that Combe must be brought up to date. What they needed most was modern accommodation for guests at the frequent weekend house-parties which were so much a feature of the lives of the Victorian élite. The agricultural recession in the UK which would so drastically reduce the income of landowners later in the century had not yet taken hold and Craven must have thought that he could easily afford the expense of the very substantial alterations he now had in mind. At this time he was probably the richest landowner in Warwickshire, drawing an annual revenue of £37,593 from nearly 31,000 acres scattered over six counties.[13]

The very successful parterre gardens at Ashdown had been designed by William Andrews Nesfield and he was commissioned to produce plans for a new garden layout at Combe. At the same time his Old Etonian son, William Eden Nesfield, aged twenty-six, had just set up his own architectural practice and no doubt as a result of the friendship with his father Craven gave the son his first big break and let him produce plans for a new wing at Combe. These plans involved the demolition of the Elizabethan east wing and the construction of a much larger block which mostly contained bedrooms, bathrooms and dressing rooms to provide the last word in luxury for house guests. The new wing was built in red sandstone in a mock-medieval French chateau style in total contrast to the rest of the house and in many ways its construction was aesthetically a disaster. It totally unbalanced the look of what was already a very uneven house, it reduced the building to a construction site for at least five years, it was not finished by the time Craven died and it cost the best part of £60,000. Showing signs of some input from the famous Richard Norman Shaw, who became Nesfield's partner, the completed east wing, based on the study of plans and old photographs, has been described rather kindly as:

..... a powerful essay in romantic medievalism. There was an impressive elevation to the east, overlooking a re-created formal garden, with an arcade on the ground floor and ranks of mullioned and transomed windows surmounted by deep-pitched roofs of French provenance. The new building derived much of its effect from a 'moat'…dug along the south front of the new house, with a boathouse at basement level.[14]

In fact the best feature of the new Combe were the gardens laid out by Nesfield senior, who constructed an impressive rectangular canal leading from the south front all the way down to the distant lake and surrounded it with pergolas, summer houses and formal parterre gardens, the details of which were implemented by Craven's head gardener, William Miller. To the north of the house some 75 great 'Wellingtonia' trees (*sequoiadendra gigantica*) were planted as part of a pleasure garden complex. Additions to the outbuildings included a new block to provide staff quarters, sited at the rear of the new east wing and a newly-designed kitchen remodelled by the painter Albert Moore, while Nesfield junior himself designed the culinary utensils. Extensions were made to the Georgian stable-block, including a new coach house and hay-loft, clad with Nesfield's trademark decorative tiles and embellished with the Craven coat-of-arms on the gable end. Finally, on the roof of this new stable block a clock tower was constructed, together with a dove-cote.[15]

Nesfield's work at Combe began in 1862 and was not entirely finished until 1870. Meanwhile the 1860s proved to be tragic years for the Craven family. Emily Mary's mother died in 1863 and Frederick Craven died of an alcohol-related illness in the following year. Then came the devastating news of the death of 'Uffie', William, Viscount Uffington, the Cravens' son and heir, aged 27. He had joined the Grenadier Guards in 1858 and accompanied the Prince of Wales on a visit to Canada two years later, but succumbed to an illness from which he died at home in April 1865. On top of this the Cravens' youngest son, Robert, who was a midshipman in the Royal Navy, mysteriously died from unrecorded causes on board his ship, HMS 'Spiteful' off Montevideo on 5 March 1866 aged sixteen.[16] The Cravens' five daughters fared less tragically: all were married, one to the son of a marquess and three to the sons of earls while four of them lived well into their eighties. All these brides would have taken with them a hefty dowry, a significant drain on the family finances.

The younger Nesfield produced a volume of architectural drawings in 1862 which he entitled 'Specimens of Medieval Architecure' and dedicated to Craven, his patron. This may have given Craven himself the idea of producing a handsome album of his own photographs and he commissioned Nesfield to design its outer covers in morocco leather with elaborate metal fittings, as well as its title page, all in medieval style. Entitled 'A Record of the Earl of Craven's Photographic Experiments' the album contained 109 of his best images and he worked on it in conjunction with his photographer daughter, Emily, especially when he began to suffer from another bout of ill-health in 1866, possibly brought on by the double blows of the deaths of his sons. With Emily he travelled on the first of August by train to Scarborough, already a fashionable seaside resort well-known for its healthy air and which he had been in the habit of visiting for some years. Soon after his arrival he suffered a third stroke and was paralysed down one side: over the next few days he appeared to make a recovery but on 25 August he collapsed and died, aged 57. The funeral took place at Combe on the first of September surrounded by what his Clarendon sister-in-law described as 'wretched scenes of misery'.[17]

The unexpected death of the unmarried 'Uffie' meant that it was his younger brother, George, who succeeded as the third Earl of Craven in 1866. His Old Etonian father did not send him to Eton in the early 1850s perhaps because his kinsman Edward Hawtrey had by then ceased to be headmaster, while the reforming headmaster of Harrow, Charles Vaughan, enjoyed a very high reputation at that time and raised the number of boys in the school from 70 to 450 during his 'reign' of fifteen years. Moreover George's uncle, Robert Grimston, a famous cricketer, was at the time an influential old boy of the school. In fact, growing criticism of outdated curricula and chaotic discipline at the famous public schools, especially Eton, led to the appointment in 1861 of a Royal Commission chaired by Craven's brother-in-law, Lord Clarendon. His report famously identified nine 'great schools' and recommended many reforms, especially that modern subjects such as science and history should be taught rather than simply the classics. No doubt the two brothers-in-law had many a chat about their ideas on how the schools of the future should be shaped. The photographer earl would presumably have been in favour of science being taught and probably practical subjects as well.

The new Earl of Craven was by now 25 and he had served in the army as a lieutenant in the Scots Fusilier Guards before promotion to captain in 1864. He lost no time in finding a suitable bride in Evelyn Barrington, aged nineteen, the second daughter of George Barrington, who had just become a Conservative MP. The marriage took place in 1867, the year in which the bride's father succeeded as the seventh Viscount Barrington in the peerage of Ireland – which meant he could remain in the Commons. He later became a privy councillor and held a number of junior ministerial posts in subsequent Conservative governments. In 1880 he was created a UK peer (as Baron Shute).

George Craven could have continued with his army career or used his seat in the Lords to advance political ambitions but apart from serving as lord-lieutenant of Berkshire for two years at the end of his life his main occupations were his family, field sports and the maintenance of his estates. His mother, now the dowager countess, lived until 1901 and being a woman of decided character and views she would have been a considerable influence on his life, at least until several years into his marriage. She did not move to Hamstead Lodge, which after the death of the previous dowager countess in 1860 was rented out to

George, the third Earl of Craven (1841-1883) died young but gave his name to his favourite brand of tobacco, 'Craven A'. He was a keen horticulturist and encouraged his head gardener, William Miller, to remodel the gardens at Combe. (NPG)

the Marquess of Donegal, who remained there until 1883. He was not a very good tenant and the locals complained that the house and the surrounding park were falling into a poor state of repair.[18]

Ashdown House was still a very attractive place in which to raise a family, while Combe would soon be released from the clutches of the younger Nesfield and his modernisation schemes. George was a lover of country pursuits, so he was content to follow in the Craven pattern of hunting, shooting, fishing and coursing. One important development concerning the Craven holdings was the decision in 1869 to sell the Stokesay estate in Shropshire with about six thousand acres to John Allcroft, a London-based glove manufacturer. The castle itself had suffered from a fire in 1830 and was in a poor state, so Allcroft built himself a new house nearby (Stokesay Court) and took the decision to conserve the medieval buildings because of their historic importance and interest. The decision to sell suggests that the Craven finances were already under strain, probably because of the great expense of the new work at Combe. This was despite the fact that in 1875 a government survey found that the Earl of Craven was the second largest landowner in Berkshire, with holdings of 19,225 acres – not including his possessions elsewhere. The Craven connection with the Stokesay area of Shropshire is still maintained through the relatively recent town of Craven Arms which was originally centred on a public house of that name and grew to be a market town after the arrival of the railway in the middle of the century.

Based at the two country houses at Ashdown and Combe, Evelyn Craven gave birth to a family of four boys and two girls over the next seventeen years. It may well have been the intention of George's father that the whole of the ancient part of Combe should be demolished and that the Nesfield east wing was only the beginning of a grand plan to turn Combe into a vast mock-medieval chateau. But his death and the consequent shortage of funds put paid to that idea. In any case, the Nesfield additions were not much liked by contemporaries, being considered by many observers to be out of character and in dubious taste.

George was more interested in horticulture than architecture and he made some important changes to the gardens and park with the help of his able head gardener, William Miller. He continued with the scheme for the planting of the 'Wellingtonias' and laid out a number of drives within the park as well as planting Lebanese cedar and rhododendron bushes, a favourite late Victorian feature. To the north-east of the house an extensive greenhouse and nursery complex was developed, surrounded by a 20ft-high wall 100 yards long by 80 yards wide. This contained 'lean-to' greenhouses for exotic fruits such as peaches, nectorines and apricots and even bananas, pineapples and grapes. In all William Miller planted about forty acres of garden, less than a quarter of which now survive – though the Wellingtonias still stand, as was intended, as a lasting memorial to the great Duke of Wellington wherever they were planted in the UK. Other aspects of the estate at Combe were supervised by the head gamekeeper, Joseph Green, the wood-ranger, Gavin Hill and the back yard manager, Thomas Reeves.[19]

According to historians of the Carreras Tobacco Company, established by Don José Carreras Ferrer in London in the early years of the nineteenth century, it was George Craven who eventually gave his name to one of the world's most famous cigarettes. Don José's son was an expert blender of tobacco and one of his customers was George Craven, for whom he created a special blend of tobacco for his pipes and cigars. Cigarettes became popular in the 1880s and in 1921 Carreras launched a brand of cigarettes called 'Craven A' which were made from the blend formerly enjoyed by George. Their originality stemmed from the fact that they were the first machine-made cork-tipped cigarettes, advertised as being less of a danger to the throat than the conventional type. They became an immediate hit in the UK and have been sold around the world in huge numbers ever since.[20]

Chapter Six

The American heiress

When George Craven was appointed lord-lieutenant of Berkshire in 1881 it might have seemed that the stage was set for a stable and dignified period in the life of the Craven family. He was happily married with six young children, living in two fine houses and still a great landowner. Unfortunately his health had always been suspect and he died at Ashdown in December 1883 aged only 42. This left his widow, Evelyn, to take care of the children, including the fourth earl, William, who was a few days short of his fifteenth birthday and still at school.

Death duties at this point were imposed at the relatively light rate of 3% on personal property only, so the financial implications of George's death were not too serious. However the UK was in the grip of a major agricultural depression which lasted from about 1873 to 1896 and which drastically reduced the income of landowners. In essence this was caused by the collapse in the price of grain imported into the UK after the market was flooded by cheap corn from the vast American prairies, transported rapidly by new railways to US ports and from there by fast new steamships. Grain prices in the UK dropped from 56 shillings a quarter in the late 1860s to as little as 22 shillings in the mid-1890s and the number of male agricultural labourers declined by a third as they moved to factories in the towns to find work. The advantage of this was that Britain became one of the leading industrialised nations but the downside, not unwelcome to socialists, was a sharp decline in the incomes of the landed classes.

Some aristocratic families in Britain discovered that a convenient way out of any financial difficulties was to marry into a rich

American family. A great many of these had been created in the United States since the end of the Civil War by entrepreneurs who made the most of opportunities offered by a rapidly expanding economy in an age of new technologies. One such entrepreneur was Bradley Martin who came from a family already wealthy through banking. Having fought on the Union side in the Civil War he married Cornelia Sherman, a friend of the Vanderbilts and herself a wealthy heiress and he pursued a successful career as a financier and industrialist in Albany. The Martins had two sons, followed by a daughter, born in 1877 and named Cornelia after her mother. In 1884, though his main home was in New York, Martin leased from the Earl of Seafield his 60,000 acre Balmacaan estate, near Inverness and very much enjoyed life on a great sporting estate, holding frequent shooting parties at Balmacaan House which were attended by the cream of society and even Russian royalty.

The young Earl of Craven, having completed his education and proved himself a fine shot was invited to one of these parties in 1892 where he was introduced to the Martins' only daughter, Cornelia. A whirlwind romance followed, resulting in marriage between the two in April 1893 when the groom was 24 and the bride a mere sixteen. The wedding took place in New York City at Grace Church on Broadway, a fine Gothic revival building belonging to the Episcopalian church. Riches were showered upon the pair by a proud father who allegedly settled a million dollars (then worth around £200,000) on Cornelia as well as a fine pearl necklace worth £12,000: meanwhile the wedding presents were valued at £40,000. The 'New York Times' commented on 11 April:

> Two interesting features of this coming international wedding are the bride's age and her jewels. Miss Cornelia Martin not long ago passed her sixteenth birthday, although in looks and actions she is two years older. The venerable grandmother of Lord Craven has

given to Miss Martin her ancestral jewels, which are of great value. At the wedding the bride will wear some of these celebrated jewels.[1]

The arrival home of the newly-wedded pair at Combe Abbey was celebrated by a party for 200 guests, while the estate tenants clubbed together to present them with a handsome silver bowl. The following night there was a big party in the indoor tennis court for all the estate workers.[2]

The Bradley-Martins, as the new countess's parents were generally known, were accustomed to giving lavish parties. Four hundred guests attended a ball at their New York home in 1885, an event which put them, in the opinion of New York society, in the same league as the Vanderbilts. Five years later, they hosted a dinner-dance for 300 guests at Delmonico's restaurant in the city. On 10 February 1897 Mrs Bradley-Martin, flanked by her daughter the Countess of Craven, was the hostess at what she and her husband were determined would be the best New York party of all time. It was held at the recently-opened Waldorf Hotel and guests were invited to dress as historical kings and queens from 1500 to 1800. The Waldorf was decorated in the style of Versailles and Bradley Martin himself appeared as Louis XIV while his wife, whom the press described as being a plump matron with blue eyes, a bow mouth and a generous bosom, as Mary, Queen of Scots. About fifty ladies dressed as Marie Antoinette, Louis XVI's fateful queen, while John Jacob Astor came as Henry of Guise and John Pierpont Morgan as Molière.

Around 1,200 invitations were sent out, though only about 700 people attended the ball, some for quite a short time because it started at 10.30 pm and went on for most of the night. The newspapers were full of details about the event long before it happened, printing lists of the invitees and the personages they were to represent. Antique shops were pillaged for suitable jewellery and ornaments and local dressmakers and tailors worked round the clock to create historically accurate costumes. The Bradley-Martins had said that they hoped the ball would give employment to people in New York and raise the profile of the city, but at a time when the average man's wage was $400 a year (about £80) the huge cost of the ball – around $370,000 – was considered an outrage by many public commentators, especially pastors from various religious denominations. According to the 'New York Times' the event was 'the most elaborate private entertainment that has ever taken place in the metropolis', while the 'New York World' calculated that the total wealth of 86 of the guests amounted to 'more than men could grasp'.[3]

The public criticism of the Bradley-Martins was so fierce that the authorities felt obliged to increase their tax bill and the couple thought it wise to retire to Scotland until the fuss died down. Given that the New York ball was held in February, Cornelia Craven's gown must have been designed to hide the fact that she was several months pregnant because on 31 July she gave birth at Combe to a son who would be her only child, inevitably named William, though also George and Bradley.

When he took his seat in the House of Lords, which he was eligible to do after his twenty-first birthday in December 1889, Cornelia's husband chose to align himself with the Liberal Party. Unlike most of his ancestors he showed an interest in developing a political career and in his early years he served as ADC to the lord lieutenant of Ireland. In 1908 the Liberals came to power under Herbert Asquith and one of the most important Acts passed by this administration was the Parliament Act of 1911 which made a revolutionary change to the British constitution by depriving the House of Lords of its veto over parliamentary bills. The need for this had arisen because the Lords rejected the government's budget in 1909 which proposed significantly increased taxation of the rich in order to finance welfare programmes for the poor. A general election in 1910

William, the fourth Earl of Craven, (1868-1921) in his robes as a peer. Unlike most of his family he was interested in politics and was a junior minister in Asquith's Liberal government, as well as being very active in local affairs. He was very popular and his death by drowning was a great shock to his many friends.

supported the government and the Lords passed the budget but Asquith used this opportunity to introduce a bill by which the Lords in future would only be able to delay finance bills for one month and other bills for two years. The Lords resisted this throughout 1910, even after another election in December supported the government. Eventually, Asquith persuaded the new king, George V, to announce that he would create enough new peers to pass the bill (about 400) and faced with this threat the Lords gave way and the bill became law in August 1911.

It is clear that the Earl of Craven played an influential role in these important events because in 1911 Asquith appointed him to the office of 'Captain of the Yeoman of the Guard' which in effect meant that he was a senior Whip in the House of Lords, responsible for persuading as many peers as possible to vote in favour of the government and for speaking at the despatch box in defence of government policy. As the Whips were usually popular and respected men chosen for their powers of persuasion through tact and charm, it follows that Craven had made a favourable impact on his contemporaries in the political world. In 1913 he was appointed lord lieutenant of Warwickshire and he continued to serve in the Whips' office until 1915. He was also very active in local affairs and took a great interest in the civic politics of Coventry, to the point where he considered standing as a Liberal candidate in local elections. He was president of the Coventry and Warwickshire Hospital Board, a justice of the peace and president of the local Territorial Association, as well as being a prominent supporter of the Warwickshire Agricultural Society: he also continued to enjoy field sports, especially partridge shoots. All this made him very popular, even loved, in Warwickshire.[4]

He was also the first head of his family who was able to take advantage of the development of the motor car. Horse-drawn vehicles had been the normal form of domestic transport up to then and the Cravens had many of these, the prize item being their Hooper-bodied state coach. But in 1896 the Daimler manufacturing company was founded and established its factory in Coventry, which made Daimler motor cars an obvious choice for Craven. By 1907 he had at least four of them, all painted in dark blue with white and red coach lining and in the summer of that year he added a fifth, a Type TP 45 10.6 litre four-seat tourer, delivered straight from the Coventry factory. He obviously liked it because the car travelled well over four thousand miles in the first year and 22,000 by 1915. In 2012, in a superb state of repair and still going strong, it sold at auction in London for £359,000.[5]

Craven was too old to train for war service but he served as a King's Messenger, which involved carrying important documents from the government to their destination at home or abroad. He also helped to raise £31,000 from charitable donations for the Prince of Wales Relief Fund for serving soldiers, himself being a significant donor, and at the end of the war he was awarded the OBE. He was a keen sailor and he took his yacht 'Sylvia' to Cowes for the annual regatta in the summer of 1921. It seems that he spent the evening with friends at the Royal Yacht Squadron and then returned to the yacht but the next morning his cabin was found to be empty and the following day his body was washed ashore two miles away. He was 52 years old. The coroner returned a verdict of accidental death but the whole episode was deeply shocking to the family and to Craven's very many friends and admirers. The funeral took place at Stockbridge Church and his body rests in a mausoleum constructed by his widow in Hamstead Marshall churchyard.[6]

The destiny of the Craven estate now lay in the hands of the former countess, Cornelia, and her only child, who succeeded as the fifth earl. The main problem confronting them was the need to pay a very large sum in death duties because the Finance Act of 1894 had modernized the previous system and also increased the tax to 7% on an estate worth between a quarter and half a million pounds, rising to

Cornelia Martin was the daughter of an exceptionally rich American father and she married the fourth Earl of Craven in New York when she was sixteen and he was twenty-four, bringing new money and glamour to the Craven family.

8% if over a million. The family still owned many thousands of acres as well as Combe Abbey, Ashdown House, Hamstead Lodge and a house in Mayfair which Cornelia had inherited from her parents.

The Great War radically changed life for the aristocracy, partly because it gave rise to a spirit of socialism and led to a marked increase in income tax and death duties, a rise in domestic and agricultural wages and a resulting scarcity of the labour needed to staff large houses. Cornelia, who was no doubt the main influence in all family decisions, decided that although Ashdown House and Hamstead Lodge would be retained, the Mayfair house and Combe Abbey must go. She herself decided to move into Hamstead Lodge, where her mother had lived from 1916 to 1920 and she transferred to it some of the best fireplaces and fittings from Combe. An impressive house in the Georgian style, the Lodge was furnished with many of the Craven pictures as well as the French 'Louis' style furniture so beloved of the American super-rich at the time. Cornelia migrated there with twenty-four indoor staff and nineteen gardeners, together with Marie-Antoinette's emeralds and china and the Empress Eugenie's jewels which had been collected by her mother. She lived at Hamstead Lodge in style until her death in 1961, visited by royalty, prominent politicians and other movers and shakers, a 'grande dame' with a pronounced American accent.

Chapter Seven

Coombe after the Cravens

The John Gray era

Following the decision of Cornelia and her son to sell the Coombe Abbey estate, which was by now spelt with two 'o's to reflect its popular pronunciation, it was offered on the market with nearly 7,000 acres and according to one authority it was:

> ....purchased by a syndicate of local professional men among whom was Samuel Corton of Leamington (he was the nominee) and Charles Band, the senior partner in a firm of Coventry solicitors. A short time later it was bought by John Todd, retired auctioneer from Northallerton, for £213,000. They were all property dealers out to make a profit. At the fourth earl's death the estate was valued at c £316,000. What did the syndicate 'pick it up' for? [1]

The contents of the house had to be sold before it was handed over to the new owners and George Lovett and Sons of Coventry were employed to supervise the sale of the contents, which took place over eight days, starting on Wednesday 4 July 1923 – American Independence Day. There were 2,277 lots consisting mostly of furniture and books from the very large Craven library. Only a few pictures, including one Rubens, were on offer.

Once the sale of the house's contents was over, John Todd, whose solicitor was Charles Band, then instructed Wintertons and

Sons of Lichfield to arrange a sale of the entire estate, which was divided into 166 lots and disposed of in two sales, on August 17 and 24. Coombe Abbey itself, with 186 acres of gardens, parkland and woods was offered as lot 126, while lot 127 consisted of the 260-acre deer park, ninety-acre lake, Menagerie House and West Lodge. Lot 128 was the seed park of 117 acres, lot 129 was 32 acres of plantation and reservoir, while lot 130 offered the East Lodge and garden. These lots came up at the second sale and the deer park was bought but the other lots were withdrawn because bids were too low. In subsequent negotiations Mr John G. Gray, a Coventry builder, bought the house and grounds for £38,000, 'plus accompanying lots and a thousand acres of farm land'. [2]

John Gray, by now in early middle-age, was a very successful businessman who had an increasing interest in farming. Originally from Lincolnshire, he moved to Coventry as a young man and with hard work and enterprise he developed a successful building business for which he became much respected in the city. His first major contract was the construction of the Courtauld factory in Coventry and he followed this with shrewd purchases of land on which he built many properties, drawing considerable income from these over several years. He fully intended to live in Coombe Abbey with his family and is even said to have bought it because he feared that, like many other country houses at the time, it might otherwise have been demolished entirely.

Even so, Gray, an experienced builder, did not shrink from demolishing about half the existing house. The whole of Nesfield's work was pulled down, leaving only the ground floor of the east wing as a ruin, which seems a strange decision – why not take it all away and construct a lawn in its place? Even Winde's fine wing was truncated: the north pavilion, which had once housed the Craven library, disappeared completely and the roof line was lowered on the remaining section by dismantling the attics and chimneys. Gray made what was

The west front of Coombe Abbey as it looked after its new owner, John Gray, demolished about half of William Winde's 1680s range and reduced the roof-line of the rest in the 1920s. He also demolished most of Nesfield's Victorian Gothic part of the house, which had stood for barely fifty years.

left of this west wing into his main living area by reconstructing the interior to a very considerable extent, switching rooms round and lowering ceilings. Out of doors, a fountain was placed in the cloister garden and a lawn and cherry trees were planted where once Nesfield's servants' quarters had stood, while the indoor real tennis court was used as a granary. Before making all these alterations, Gray stripped out most of the valuable interior fittings such as antique fireplaces and panelling, which together with ornamental features from the gardens were sold for considerable sums, defraying some of the cost of the house's purchase.[3]

No doubt those who knew and loved the house in the Craven period were horrified by these developments and architectural historians have not been kind to Mr Gray, one of them describing his efforts as 'an act of architectural vandalism hard to match in the history of the Warwickshire country house', leaving Coombe Abbey 'a meaningless torso'.[4] But John Gray considered that he had reduced the house to a manageable size for the times while still retaining some very fine features and he lived happily there with his family for nearly twenty years, keeping a close eye on the two local farms in his ownership. In due course he became famous for his herd of 'Abbeycombe' red poll cattle and he was also considered to be an authority on paintings, silverware, porcelain and antiques in general.[5]

As for the areas adjoining the house, the deer park was bought in the 1923 sale by a syndicate headed by Mr William Lindley, a solicitor from Coventry whose main aim was to prevent it from being developed and it remained parkland. Mr Lindley also bought the Menagerie House and some eighty acres which he renamed 'Woodlands' and he created a fine rock-garden there using some of the red sandstone from the demolished parts of Coombe Abbey. Nine acres overlooking the lake were bought by Mr Sydney Penn, who built a house there, while Mr Albert Ward bought West Lodge and six acres. In 1934 the Coventry city authorities began discussions with Rugby District Council about acquiring the acres round Coombe Abbey for use as a public park and in 1938 a price was negotiated with Mr Lindley and the other members of the consortium for the sale of the deer park for public use.[6] With the outbreak of war in 1939 these negotiations were put on hold and officers and men of the Royal Artillery were billeted around the walled garden and farm buildings of the Abbey. The Gray family remained at the house and entertained the troops from time to time with dances and parties in the North Parlour. After the devastating Coventry air raids of 1940 and 1941 the lake was drained in case the water might serve as a directional aid to enemy aircraft.

Seven years after the war John Gray decided to 'downsize' and moved in 1952 to a smaller house near Warwick, leasing the Abbey to the General Electric Company who used it as a hall of residence for their post-graduate employees and apprentices. A mains electricity supply was installed and a tarmacadam access drive constructed from the Binley-Brinklow road to the south entrance. The ten original students gradually increased to seventy as more rooms were brought into commission and a roof was constructed on the remaining ground floor of the Nesfield building, which then provided modern, heated accommodation for about twenty students. These very practical young apprentices were encouraged to undertake projects on the house and by 1959 they had built themselves a new swimming pool and hard tennis court to keep fit. One of them was David Motkin who was fascinated by the house he found himself occupying and set about chronicling its history, which was privately published as a forty-page booklet by the 'Coombe Abbey House Committee' in 1961. He wrote in its preface:

> From 1960 to 1961 I was privileged to live at Coombe during my apprenticeship with the GEC. I soon discovered that there was no ready source of information about the house and its history, so I

determined to remedy the situation. Having very little free time, I drew my information from a single, easily accessible archive – the Coventry and Warwickshire collection of Coventry libraries, in whose reading room I spent several hours each Saturday during the winter and early spring. Trained as a physicist, and certainly no historian, I rapidly became aware of my limited knowledge of the subject and it was with some uneasiness that I brought my text to publication that summer.[7]

Forty years later and enjoying both the luxuries of retirement and the internet, in 2003 David Motkin collaborated with his Coombe contemporary Peter Page to produce a revised and updated online edition of 'The Story of Coombe Abbey'. Of his time at the Abbey Motkin writes:

In 1961 there were seventy apprentices resident at Coombe Abbey, most of them staying there for only one year. They were supervised by a warden who lived with his family in a self-contained flat and there were also several resident domestic staff. The house was run by a house committee which was elected from the residents twice yearly and was under the chairmanship of the Warden. The committee organized social functions ... and was responsible for the organization and running of the house. It also administered a house fund to which all residents contributed a small sum each week and which was used to provide amenities not provided by the GEC. Another committee, the bar committee, ran a licensed club whose profits also went to the house fund. A 'do it yourself' attitude was encouraged in the house and almost all the apprentices spent much of their free time labouring on various projects associated with improving the amenities... [8]

Country Park and Hotel

John Gray died in 1958 and left Coombe Abbey to his daughter, Winifred, who was married to Edward Walpole-Brown. By 1963 surveys revealed that the building suffered from significant structural weaknesses and the GEC decided not to renew their lease and closed down the hostel in 1964. Faced with the possibility of very expensive repair bills, Mrs Walpole-Brown decided to put the house on the market again. This was the perfect opportunity for Coventry City Council to complete a long campaign for a public park, which had been a cherished aim since the 1930s. The agreement made in 1938 with the various owners of the deer park was put into effect in the early 1950s, then in 1958 the council was able to buy the lake, its fishing rights and the surrounding woodland, some 110 acres, for £28,500. Now its offer of £36,000 for the house and a further 150 acres was accepted and this was enough to make the idea of a country park become a reality. [9]

Between 1964 and 1966 the council spent £19,000 on dredging the eastern part of the lake, building lavatories and a small cafeteria and laying out a car park: also the 'home-made' GEC swimming pool and tennis court were removed and the area made into lawns. On 14 May 1966, a warm and sunny day, the Lord Mayor of Coventry, Councillor Edwin Rogers, formally opened the 250-acre 'Coombe Abbey Regional Park' an event that reportedly attracted 60,000 visitors. In 1968 the Countryside Act made it possible for the council to apply for government grants in areas committed to the preservation of natural beauty and in 1970 the official name 'Coombe Country Park' was adopted. Boating facilities were provided on part of the lake, nature trails were laid out and a bird park established. In 1974, after the death of William Lindley, the council was able to acquire 'Woodlands' and a further 88 acres.[10]

After being diagnosed with serious structural problems in 1964 Coombe Abbey itself was given emergency repair treatment by the council but otherwise it was closed to the public and left unoccupied while attention focused on the park. But it was a listed building for which the council bore responsibility so in 1971 it was leased to Historic Productions Ltd who staged very popular 'medieval banquets' on the ground floor of the west wing and in the 'Great Parlour' in the north wing. Some ten years later the indoor tennis court was converted into a public house called 'The Granary' to reflect its most recent use. The main problem for the council was the apparently never-ending need to repair and maintain the fabric of the main house. In 1976 some £25,000 was spent on reconstruction of three of the western gables and one on the south side while in 1983 the roof of the south-west range was repaired, the centre south gable and window were rebuilt and a million-pound programme of further extensive repairs was planned and carried out over the next five years.[11]

At this point Robin Moore, the head ranger of the Country Park, published a history of Coombe Abbey which he had been working on for some time. Born in Coventry in 1950 he was employed at the park from 1975 and recalled one day 'turning into the entrance to Coombe Abbey, the long tarmac driveway stretching out ahead of me, straight as a die for almost half a mile… Pointing my car in the familiar direction of the abbey I began to day-dream. Why, I wondered, did they ever stop using the old entrance and driveway? You see, I knew that two hundred years ago the house was approached from a completely different direction'.[12] He decided to do his own research into the history of the house and its owners and although he claimed he was not a historian, his work was thorough and the book gained greatly from his own professional knowledge of the estate and its gardens.

Meanwhile, Coventry City Council became more and more aware of the size and potential expense of the task of maintaining Coombe Abbey in a viable state and in 1988 they decided to look for an organization which would develop the Abbey in a partnership deal. In 1991 an agreement was clinched with the 'No Ordinary Hotels' Group and 'Try Construction' by which all three parties committed themselves to major financial investment at Coombe Abbey. This would involve an ambitious rebuilding of the existing house to create a hotel with a historic feel to it yet equipped with all the modern amenities expected of a luxury hotel.

When this became public knowledge, there was panic in some quarters. 'Another Alton Towers?' asked the *Rugby Advertiser* in September, and the Rugby Conservative MP Jim Pawsey launched a vitriolic attack on the scheme, denouncing Coventry City Council's expansionist plans as 'the octopus of civic imperialism'. In reply, it was explained that the Abbey was 'crippled with disease' and needed more money than the council could afford on its own to save the site.[13] Soon enough excited rumours began to spread that the Communist Government of China as well as financial backers in Saudi Arabia were prepared to put millions into the venture, in the same way that Lumley Castle, another historic property owned by the 'No Ordinary Hotels' group near Newcastle had allegedly raised finance outside Europe.

In fact the scheme went ahead in 1993 and a large modern visitors centre was constructed out of sight of the main house in a park which by now consisted of 372 acres and had already become a much-loved part of the lives of the citizens of Coventry and many people beyond. On 6 September 1993 the *Coventry Evening Telegraph* was able to report:

> A £2.3 million visitors centre and car park have already been built as part of a package between the Coventry City Council, Try Construction Group and No Ordinary

Hotels. Now detailed plans for the construction and extension of the abbey and real tennis court buildings into a 64-bed hotel and conference area, with an adjacent 171-bay car park will appear before Rugby Borough Council's planning committee tomorrow for approval.[14]

In fact the planning committee had its doubts and decided that they wanted to visit the site to see what impact the new scheme would have before making a decision. The main area of concern was the intention to build a new block on top of what remained of the Nesfield ground floor in a style reminiscent of Nesfield's yet providing all the modern amenities needed for a 64 bedroom hotel. To save costs this would be built out of reconstituted stone instead of the real thing, a plan that did not go down well with a number of 'heritage' watchdogs. The secretary of the Ancient Monuments Society told the committee that 'if listed building consent is given, all those involved in listed building procedures might as well give up' arguing that the scheme 'would seriously damage the historic integrity and visual pleasure to be had at this Grade I listed building'. English Heritage, though not seeking to block the scheme, nevertheless found the plans 'architecturally disappointing'.[15]

As the Rugby planning committee dragged its feet, Gordon Bear, the entrepreneur businessman who was the driving force behind Lumley Castle and 'No Ordinary Hotels', told a local paper that:

All in all some two and a half years have been spent in extensive discussions and negotiations about the Coombe project. It is sad to see those who have recently criticized our proposals seem to be doing so from a totally selfish viewpoint. English Heritage do recognize the importance of the commercial considerations, hence their willingness to recommend the scheme ....[16]

In the end the planning committee approved the scheme unanimously early in October 1993, with the important proviso that only natural stone was to be used in the construction of the new hotel block.

The council set up a board to be responsible for developing Coombe Abbey which consisted of members of the council and representatives from 'No Ordinary Hotels' and 'Try Construction'. The first move was the opening of a new banqueting centre by the conversion of the former Abbeygate medieval banqueting hall. Then hand-painted fragments of a 1650s ceiling were discovered in the main house and work had to be halted until they were properly conserved. Plans for two golf courses, a club house, restaurant, bar and parking ran into strong opposition from a host of garden and country park preservation societies and wild life trusts and they had to be dropped. Meanwhile 300,000 people visited the park in 1993, and half a million was the target for 1994.[17]

Try Construction spent about sixteen months building the new hotel block, which retained some Nesfield features such as the moat and boathouse and solid arcades at ground level. The rest of the block more or less replaced the Nesfield building that John Gray had largely demolished, but it was not as high and had fewer 'Gothic' features. Inside, the design was by no means ultra-modern but aimed at a compromise between the past and the present. The *Coventry Evening Telegraph* announced early in January 1995 that the new 'Coombe Abbey Hotel' would open on 17 February when the first bedrooms of the 'luxury £17 million hotel' would be unveiled, having 'four-poster beds, lavish drapes, tasselled curtains and en-suite bathrooms – a far cry from religious denial'. It added that the cost of enjoying these new facilities would be £95 a night, excluding breakfast. When the hotel opened and journalists were able to see for themselves the new complex with its magnificent Cloisters restaurant, relatively unchanged from the time of William Winde, its Chapter House bar and private dining

The modern wing built by Try Construction for 'No Ordinary Hotels' in 1994 on the footprint of the original Nesfield building, most of which had been demolished by John Gray in the 1920s. The moat, arch and ground floor are original Nesfield but the rest has been built in a sympathetic style while providing the modern amenities necessary for a luxury hotel.

room, they described Coombe Abbey's 'eccentric new identity, half gothic film-set, half gold-plated playground for the seriously well-off' and were amused by a mischievous line of three mock-medieval tombs down the main corridor. 'The mixture of original and fake is bewildering' they found, 'it is almost a shock to realize that the sandstone arches in the ceiling are solid stone, features of the earliest surviving parts of the abbey.'[18]

Towards the end of 1995 the hotel was nominated for the local paper's 'Business of the Year Award' on the grounds that it had already created seventy-five full time and fifty part-time jobs as well as attracting major clients in the lucrative conference and exhibition market. By now its 63 bedrooms were fully operational and the number of visitors had increased by a quarter in two years. A local paper also stated that the total cost of the new hotel had been £17.5 million, including grants worth £1.2 million from the European Economic Community.[19] In December 1996 a headline announced 'Booming Hotel to Expand', explaining that a twenty-bedroom extension costing £1million would open in the spring of 1998 and the hotel proudly claimed that more than 100,000 people had been customers since its opening and that some two hundred full and part-time jobs had been created. The twenty new bedrooms were located in an extension built onto the north-east part of the existing east wing and were in fact ready for use in July 1999. By this time the real tennis court had been converted for use as a well-equipped conference centre.[20]

In 2009 the hotel made another major move forward when a completely new 40-bedroom complex in a well-mannered brick design was built to the north of the main hotel and a large 'Conservatory Restaurant' was constructed on the north side of the main east wing. The building which contained the extra rooms was an ambitious and expensive addition which was financed through a bank loan but unfortunately the financial crisis of the next few years had a serious impact on the hotel's trade and in 2013, according to local media, the council 'bought out the then struggling hotel's £6.5 million bank loan. The council took over as mortgage lender to the privately-owned medieval-themed hotel, which could then borrow at much cheaper interest rates.'[21] After this the financial situation steadily improved, the hotel met its borrowing requirements and in 2016 an attractive summerhouse in the hotel's garden was refurbished for use as a wedding venue. Meanwhile the Country Park was modernized and developed under a five-year management plan, details of which were set out in a very comprehensive survey published in 2012.

Then on 8 October 2017 the *Coventry Observer* broke the news that Coventry City Council were in secret discussions with the hotel to buy back the leasehold and on 24 October it announced that the hotel had been acquired for 'up to £11 million'. The council's cabinet member for jobs and regeneration told a local newspaper: 'The owner [Gordon Bear] wants to retire. He wanted us to buy it. It won't be run by the council but we will oversee it in terms of a shareholders panel, as 100% shareholder.' It was a good investment, he added, and was expected to make a ten percent return. 'We believe it is the best way to get revenue into the council for the local authority to spend on services. It will also protect our heritage and culture', he said.[22]

Although opposition members on the council denounced the purchase as a 'shady, Fawlty Towers deal' at a time when the council was cutting services elsewhere, the Labour majority argued that it made good sense to safeguard this important asset. The council was once again the freehold owner of the hotel as well as the Country Park, by now extending to 500 acres, and could expect to benefit substantially from the revenues generated by both. The managers of the hotel, meanwhile, announced that despite the change of ownership, it was 'business as usual' at the hotel. With its spectacular garden setting, its rich historical associations, fine interiors and hints of ghostly presences Coombe Abbey Hotel has brought pleasure to tens of thousands of guests and hosted thousands of weddings and other celebrations over

The formal gardens at Coombe Abbey, looking towards the lake.

nearly a quarter of a century. Its neighbouring Country Park is an enduring asset to the local population and delights that were once restricted to a small circle of aristocrats are now easily accessible to all.

An aerial photograph of Coombe Abbey Hotel. Courtesy of r/britpics.

New hotel block, 2009

Stable block, 18th & 19th c.

'Royal' Tennis Court c.1810

Rebuilt hotel in Nesfield style 1994, 1999

'Great Parlour' etc 17th c. and later

1684

1669

Site of demolished medieval abbey church leading on to the cloisters

Appendix

What happened to the Cravens?

The family history of the Earls of Craven after 1922 is in many ways a tragic one involving rows and estrangements, fatal accidents and escapades which gave rise to a good deal of public scandal and gossip. Moreover the dominating theme is the relentless dispersal of the family estates and possessions to pay for a wide range of debts, and in particular, crushing death duties. There is no official documentation of these events and this account has been put together from information in the public domain, including articles posted on the internet. Therefore it may not be entirely accurate but neither would be any account provided by members of the family, even if they were prepared to be interviewed on the subject.

The only real cloud in the domestic life of the fourth Earl of Craven and his American wife Cornelia was the boisterous behaviour of their son and only child, William George Bradley, Viscount Uffington, who was born in 1897, the year of the celebrated New York party. According to a detailed internet article that was posted in 2012 he was sent to Eton but expelled for high jinks in a four-wheeled cab outside Windsor Castle. He continued his schooling in Eastbourne but after dinner one night, and still in his evening clothes, he shinned up local gas lamp posts and put several lamps out. Unfortunately he was spotted by a policeman who refused his offer to relight them and arrested him. Later he joined the special reserve of the Hampshire regiment but then attended a theatrical performance in Ryde, on the Isle of Wight, and threw eggs at one of the actors from his box, as a result of which he was disciplined by a military court. Meanwhile, two of his fellow officers encouraged him to gamble for very high stakes and he lost considerable sums. Stationed in Portsmouth he again went on a spree putting out gas lights and fled from the police on a motorbike, only to crash into a motor car so seriously that he was badly injured and spent a considerable time in hospital.

In Portsmouth he fell in love with a chorus girl whose next show was in Birmingham, so he told his military superiors that he needed dental treatment in London and rode up to Birmingham on his motorbike to see her. He had little cash with him so slept in a public park all night and 'acquired' a bottle of perfume from a shop to give to the girl. When she moved on to Liverpool, he followed on his bike but was discovered by an agent working for his father. He was escorted back to barracks and again subjected to military discipline. Eventually he was posted to Bermuda but insisted on climbing the smoke stack of the steamer on the way.[1]

When Europe went to war in August 1914 he was still only seventeen and training with his regiment for active service in a camp near Balmacaan, the Scottish estate owned by his grandparents the Bradley-Martins. There he happened to meet Mary Williamina George, the very beautiful daughter of the town clerk of Invergordon and he fell in love and persuaded her to marry him. Despite the fact that this was not necessarily a match they would have chosen, his parents put a brave face on it and accepted their new daughter-in-law with good grace. The wedding took place in 1916 and after the honeymoon William returned to his duties as a lieutenant in the third battalion of the Hampshire regiment, where he had every opportunity to make use of his natural vitality and taste for danger and excitement. Unfortunately he was very badly wounded in action, losing one leg and having his right arm shattered. He survived as a war hero and a son and heir, named William, was born to his wife in 1917. Mainly as a result of gambling he found himself in severe financial difficulties after 1918 and was forced to file for bankruptcy, owing tens of thousands of pounds. He also lost interest in his wife and instead pursued other women, notably Vera, Countess Cathcart, with whom he eloped to the French Riviera and later her native South Africa. A scandalised Lord Cathcart divorced Vera in 1922 and she lived openly with William for the next three years.[2]

When his father was so tragically drowned at Cowes in 1921 William became the fifth Earl of Craven, aged 24, and one can only imagine the dialogues that subsequently took place between this wayward only child and his American mother over the future of the family estates. As we have seen, the main decision they took was the sale of Coombe Abbey and some London properties, which probably paid off the young earl's debts and the death duty bill, leaving him with Ashdown House as a family home as well as very extensive estates in Berkshire. His mother was rich in her own right, having inherited half her father's $4 million fortune after his death in 1913 and, as noted, she chose to live in considerable style in Hamstead Lodge. Her son's major concern on a personal level was the breakdown of his marriage to Williamina (known as 'Mina'), who brought widespread publicity to the family problems by suing her husband in the English courts for the restitution of conjugal rights in view of his relationships with other women. In the middle of all this William suddenly died in September 1932 from peritonitis while in Pau, in southern France, aged 35.

His son the sixth earl, christened William Robert Bradley but known as 'Bobby', was aged fifteen and still at Eton but his mother at this point followed her conscience in converting to the Roman Catholic faith, together with her son, who was moved from Eton to the Roman Catholic Downside, in Somerset. To pay the death duties now demanded there was in 1934 a sale of extensive farmland around Hamstead Marshall, in the villages of Enborne and Kintbury. After school Bobby attended the Northamptonshire Institute of Agriculture and he celebrated his twenty-first birthday in September 1938 by giving a party in Newbury for tenants and employees who presented him with a seventeenth-century clock from the time of his ancestor

The young fifth Earl of Craven (1897-1932), showing signs of his war injuries. He and his mother sold Coombe Abbey in 1923 soon after the tragic death of the fourth earl resulted in heavy death duties and other drains on the family finances. It had been in the Craven family's possession for 301 years. (NPG)

the Cavalier Earl. Then in May 1939 he made what was regarded in the family as an irresponsibly impulsive marriage to Irene Meyrick, whose father was a doctor in Kensington and whose mother had run dubious night clubs in the West End. The wedding took place quietly in London and both Bobby's mother 'Mina' and his grandmother Cornelia registered their disapproval by not attending. In January the following year Irene gave birth to a daughter, Sarah.[3]

By this time war had been declared and Bobby, who served as a second lieutenant in the Coldstream Guards, later transferred to the Royal Naval Reserve. His relationship with his wife deteriorated but because he was a Roman Catholic it was no simple matter to end the marriage and it was not until 1954 that he obtained a religious annulment and a civil divorce. Almost immediately he then married Elizabeth Johnstone-Douglas, daughter of the Scottish painter Sholto Douglas, a kinsman of the Marquess of Queensbury, and they subsequently had three children, Thomas, Ann and Simon. Ashdown House had been requisitioned by the military during the war and it was left in a derelict state after their departure, so the Cravens took the decision in 1956 to donate the building to the National Trust. They also sold thousands of acres of surrounding farmland, including the iconic ancient monument of the Uffington White Horse. Bobby was elected a member of Berkshire County Council and in 1959 he was appointed a Knight of the Sovereign Order of Malta, a Roman Catholic organization which administers charitable aid through medical professionals and volunteers in many countries of the world.[4]

The next financial blow for the family came with the death of Bobby's grandmother, Cornelia, in 1961. She had continued to live in Hamstead Lodge during the war years, when unlike many local country houses it was not requisitioned by the government, possibly because of her American citizenship. Troops were stationed in the park which was visited by General Eisenhower in May 1944 just before the D.Day invasion of Normandy. Inevitably Cornelia's lavish style of life was drastically modified during the war and after 1945 former standards of grandeur were never achieved again. She was buried in the mausoleum she had built for her husband and her estate was valued at £800,000, after she had bequeathed seven paintings to the Royal Collection and two to the National Gallery. This left death duties to be paid of £353,555 and Bobby raised most of this by selling Cornelia's famous jewels at Sotheby's for nearly £300,000. He himself moved into Hampstead Lodge with his wife and elder daughter Sarah, now 21, son Thomas, aged four, Ann, two, and baby Simon, born in September 1961. Assisted by his agent, Kenneth Banner, he set about rationalising and renovating what remained of the Craven estate, which had shrunk to about 3,000 acres from the 40,000 of the early 1890s. He also worked enthusiastically with a group of people whose aim was to re-open the Kennet and Avon canal.[5]

Sadly, he was not to enjoy the stable future with his young family that he expected and no doubt deserved because he fell ill and was diagnosed with leukaemia, which killed him in January 1965 when he was forty-seven years old. This left his elder son, Thomas, aged seven, to succeed to the title and his widow to work out how to pay another round of death duties, estimated at £250,000. She married Kenneth Banner in 1966 and they decided to downsize by moving into a newly-built large bungalow close to Hamstead Lodge called the 'Dower House', while the Lodge itself was let on a 20-year lease and opened as the 'Edgecumbe Nursing Home'. Unwanted pictures and other heirlooms from the Lodge went off to the salerooms.

Thomas, the seventh earl, went to board nearby at Douai School, run by the Benedictines at Woolhampton in Berkshire and after he reached his twenty-first birthday in 1976 he made his home in the Dower House while his mother and stepfather moved to a manor house near Pevensey in East Sussex. Between 1977 and 1978 two local sales of Craven land and property took place, disposing of two farms and eight cottages, while 159 items of gold and silver were sold at

Christie's in 1979. According to Penelope Stokes, the historian of Hamstead Marshall, Thomas's 'lifestyle was considered wild, but locally he is still remembered as a likeable lad who fell into bad company', though 'his estate-management style had given rise to concern in the village'.[6] He fathered a child by a Scottish girl and was considered by some of his friends to suffer from schizophrenia, a disorder which often distances the sufferer from reality.

In October 1983 headlines in the national papers announced that 'a 26-year old English nobleman killed himself with a shotgun because he was troubled by a centuries-old curse that all the family's menfolk would die young, according to local villagers...'[7] This shocking event took place in the house of Thomas's mother in East Sussex and inevitably gave rise to sensational speculation in many newspapers about the alleged 'curse of the Cravens', said to have been laid upon the family by a gipsy girl who in times past had been made pregnant by a former earl. One version ran that all the earls were doomed to die before their mothers, another that they would die comparatively young. Though it is not unlikely that former earls had sired illegitimate children (as indeed Thomas had done) there is no historical evidence for such a curse, and even if there were, most people would probably dismiss the effect of a curse unless it appeared to be borne out by a long-standing series of exceptional coincidences. If this happened, then psychologists might argue that a legendary curse that actually had some effect could develop into a self-fulfilling prophesy. This was clearly the line that local gossips tended to take and that many newspapers chose to expand. The fact that all of the seven earls since 1801 had died before the age of 58, and some much earlier, cannot be denied, though the photographer second earl did outlive his mother, Louisa.

The death of Thomas meant that his younger brother, Simon, also educated at Douai and now aged 22, succeeded as the eighth earl. Yet another round of death duties had to be paid and some fifty paintings were sold at Phillips in London, raising £830,000: but most of that went to the tax man and the rest to Thomas's illegitimate son. In June 1984 1,336 remaining acres of land were sold at Hamstead Marshall, this time including Hamstead Lodge, the last of the Craven family's ancestral houses.[8] In 1988 Simon married Teresa, the daughter of Arthur Downes of Black Hall, Clane, County Kildare in Ireland, and she gave birth to a son, named Benjamin, in June, 1989. Meanwhile, Simon trained to be a nurse and lived with his wife and baby in a modest house in Eastbourne but on 30 August 1990, while setting out to see his mother near Pevensey, he crashed his mini-Cooper into two parked cars on Seaside Road in Eastbourne and died from the severe head injuries he sustained, aged 28.

Inevitably, this was reported in the local Eastbourne newspaper, which announced, under the headline 'Dead Earl Laughed at Craven Curse Tale':

> The family of a former student nurse has dismissed stories that his death in a car crash last week was the result of [an ancient] curse...The 28 year-old was the eighth Earl of Craven and his death re-awoke stories of a curse on the family said to cause all its male heirs to die young. But the family solicitor said Simon ....was not scared by the legendary curse on his family. He said 'He did not believe in it. He simply laughed it off. Quite honestly, the family wished everyone would drop it... It was never heard of until a newspaper article ten years ago.' The Craven family blame the story of the curse on a secretary, sacked back in 1977, who wanted to spread gossip.[9]

Simon's mother was at this time married to Kenneth Banner and she had now lost two young sons in tragic circumstances. In 1990

Mr Banner contracted to buy Morewood House in Hamstead Marshall, together with 400 acres, and after his death in 1996 it was, according to some sources, placed in trust for the future use of the young ninth earl.[10] By 2003 Teresa was recorded as living with her son in a relatively modern house near Waldron, East Sussex, and in 2011 Simon's mother died at the age of 95, leaving eleven grandchildren, though only one male Craven – Benjamin.[11] He and his mother have guarded their privacy closely and no details of his education or way of life over the years have been divulged publicly, except the address of the present 'family seat', near Waldron.

Ashdown House

The National Trust accepts historic houses as a gift on variable terms depending on the circumstances. When Ashdown was transferred to the trust by the Cravens in 1956 as more or less an empty shell it took overall responsibility for the preservation and repair of the fabric but also leased the house to a tenant who had the exclusive right to occupy most of the building, except for the main staircase – one of its best architectural features – which gave access to the roof with magnificent views over the Berkshire Downs. An early tenant was John Goulandris, a Greek shipping magnate, but in 1984 it was leased to the businessman and philanthropist Max Ulfane and his wife, Joy. With considerable funds at their disposal they embarked upon a mission to create both a comfortable home and also a house which reflected its historic past, especially the connection with the Cavalier Earl and Elizabeth of Bohemia. Helped by interior designers such as David Mlinaric and Hugh Henry they refurnished the house with sympathetic antique furniture and paintings and acquired an important portrait of the Cavalier Earl and other members of the Craven family as well as portraits of Elizabeth of Bohemia and her children, perhaps from the sale of family pictures which followed the death of the seventh earl in 1983. Between 1990 and 1991 the architect Philip Jebb designed a Palladian-style orangery complex with a swimming pool and although the house was only open to the public at weekends and the tour was limited to the main staircase and roof, it attracted some 20,000 visitors a year.

In 2010 the Ulfanes took the decision to leave Ashdown and sent most of the contents of the house for auction at Sotheby's in London. Many admirers of both the house and its contents were dismayed by this move, but the sale went ahead on 29 October with an estimate of £1.6 million for the 363 lots. Sotheby's made much of the Craven-Elizabeth 'love story' and produced a well-illustrated catalogue entitled 'The Winter Queen and the Earl of Craven' which was full of highly desirable antique items. Meanwhile Lord Dalmeny, the deputy chairman of Sotheby's, announced that 'many great houses have stories attached, but few can tell a love story as compelling as that of Ashdown House'. The sale attracted a great deal of interest and realized £2,730,441, far more than estimated.

The Ulfanes had managed to acquire nine paintings from what must have been part of the previous Craven collection and they all fetched very high prices. A full-length van Dyke portrait of the Cavalier Earl wearing armour and holding a baton went over estimate for £133,250, and a head and shoulders study of him by Honthorst fetched more than twice the estimate, at £46,850. The only portrait of Elizabeth was a rather dull effort by 'school of Honthorst' though it realized £37,250, but there were some very fine portraits of her children. One, a self-portrait by Princess Louise, estimated at eight to twelve thousand, sold for £67,250, while a lovely study of her fetched £49,250, one of Henriette £20,000, and one of Prince Edward, Count Palatine of Simmern, £34,850 – all by Honthorst. A 'circle of van Dyke' twin portrait of two children said to be Prince Edward and Princess Henriette, realized £34,850.[12]

'An Allegory of Love' painted by Sir Peter Lely (1618–1680).

The most intriguing painting in this sale was a work by Sir Peter Lely which went for well over twice the estimate, at £70,850. The art expert Sir Oliver Miller bought it at a Sotheby's auction in 1969 for a mere £280 and the Ulfanes apparently acquired it directly from him.[13] Entitled 'An Allegory of Love' it is thought to show The Cavalier Earl and Elizabeth in a very informal setting, surrounded by three semi-naked children. In 2015 Nicola Cornick, a trained historian who worked as a guide at Ashdown for many years and who has written many successful historical novels, published 'House of Shadows', an imaginative tale centred on the house and the Craven family. For her the Cavalier Earl was an unqualified manly hero, a brave soldier and devoted courtier whose love for Elizabeth was not only consummated but bonded by decades of secret marriage. Although we have no proof that this was the case Cornick suggests that this painting by Lely is powerful evidence of the fact that a very close relationship between the two was well known and recognized by their contemporaries. She sees the three children as cupids, which are symbols of love, and notices that Craven's wrist is tied with blue ribbon, the 'cordon bleu' implying knightly chivalry and devotion. Moreover, Elizabeth has a laurel wreath in her hand and seems about to crown Craven with these laurels, symbols of marriage. It is only fair to say that in Cornick's story, Ashdown was burnt to the ground at the start of the nineteenth century, but this is the sort of licence permitted to historical novelists.[14]

With the sale over in 2010 and the house emptied, new leases were allegedly on offer for sixty years (£4.5 million) or 83 years (£5.3 million) and among those interested was the sculptor Anish Kapoor. In the end it was Pete Townshend, lead guitarist, backing vocalist and principal songwriter of the famous rock band 'The Who' who secured the lease, allegedly for £4.1 million. A structural renovation was subsequently undertaken by the National Trust and in 2014 its results were commended by the Royal Institute of Chartered Surveyors for very high standards of research and conservation. A spokeswoman for the National Trust told *Newbury Today* that Pete Townshend's lease money would have 'indirectly' paid towards the restoration. She also said 'The rental would go into a pot that helps to fund the upkeep of the property. But he wouldn't have made a direct donation – that's the responsibility of the trust.'[15] In 2018 the house and gardens remain open to the public at restricted times and it is still possible to climb to the roof up the main staircase, which has been hung with other suitable paintings from the National Trust's collection.

SOURCES

Books

Beresford, Maurice, *The Deserted Villages of Warwickshire*, in Birmingham and Midland Institute Archaeological Society Transactions and Proceedings, Vol LXVI, 1950.

Chanan, Noel, *William, Earl of Craven and the Art of Photography*, Halsgrove, 2006.

Dugdale, William, *The Antiquities of Warwickshire*, Vol I, second edition: John Osborn and Thomas Longman, 1730, reprinted by E.J.Morten, Manchester.

Fraser, Antonia, *Faith and Treason, The story of the Gunpowder Plot*, Anchor Books, 1996.

Freeland, Chrystia, *Plutocrats*, Doubleday, Canada, 2012.

Foster, Joseph, *Alumni Oxonienses, 1715-1886*, Oxford, 1888.

Gorst-Williams, Jessica, *Elizabeth, The Winter Queen*, Abelard, 1976.

Moore, Robin, *A History of Coombe Abbey*, Coventry, 1983.

Motkin, David L., *The Story of Coombe Abbey*, (1961) updated version available by searching the title under 'Coventry Walks', online.

Power, Eileen, *The Wool Trade in English Medieval History*, Oxford, 1941.

Rodwell, Warwick, *Combe Abbey: From Cistercian Abbey to Country House* in Linda Monckton and Richard K. Morris (eds.) *Coventry: Medieval Art, Archaeology and Architecture in the City and its Vicinity*, Leeds, 2011.

Rouse, W.H.D., *A History of Rugby School*, Duckworth, London, 1898.

Stokes, Penelope, *Craven Country, The Story of Hamstead Marshall*, privately printed 1996, second edition, 2012.

Tyack, Geoffrey, *Warwickshire Country Houses*, Phillimore, 1994.

Tyack, Bradley and Pevsner, *The Buildings of England: Berkshire*, Yale, 2010.

Wheatley, Henry Benjamin, *London Past and Present*, Vol 1, Cambridge, 1891.

Wilson, Harriette, *The Memoirs of Harriette Wilson*, Vol I, Eveleigh Nash, London, 1909, Gutenberg online version.

Woodward, G.W.O., *Dissolution of the Monasteries*, Blandford, 1969.

Youings, Joyce, *The Dissolution of the Monasteries*, George Allen and Unwin, 1971.

Oxford Dictionary of National Biography (ODNB), Oxford, 2004

Entries as cited in the source notes, but especially:
Smuts, R. Malcolm, *William Craven, first Earl of Craven*
Asch, Ronald G, *Princess Elizabeth Stuart*

Reference Works

Coombe Country Park Management Plan, 2012-2017, updated 2013, online
Cracroft's Peerage, (online)
Victoria County History of the County of Warwick, Vol 2, 1908

Coventry City Archives

Inventory of paintings at Combe Abbey, (1866)
Newspaper articles from local Warwickshire papers, as cited.

REFERENCE NOTES

Chapter One

1   William Dugdale, *The Antiquities of Warwickshire*, Vol 1 pp221-3 and ODNB Vol 39 pp588-590
2   ODNB Vol 36 pp359-361
3   Dugdale, p222
4   Ibid.
5   see the Victoria County History of the County of Warwick, Vol 2, pp78-81
6   Maurice Beresford, *The Deserted Villages of Warwickshire*, p83
7   Dugdale, p223,224
8   Ibid. p 224
9   Geoffrey Tyack, *Combe Abbey*, p57
10 Warwick Rodwell, *Combe Abbey*
11 Dugdale, p223
12 VCH *Warwickshire* p73
13 Eileen Power, *The Wool Trade in English Medieval History*, p20
14 Ibid. pp21,22
15 Ibid. p27
16 Ibid. pp42,43
17 Ibid. pp43,44
18 David Motkin, *The Story of Coombe Abbey*, Chapter 2
19 Ibid.
20 Robin Moore, *A History of Coombe Abbey*, p20
21 Motkin, Chapter 2
22 ODNB Vol 36 pp359-361
23 Motkin, Chapter 2
24 Sybil M. Jack, *Dissolution Dates, etc*, Wiley Online Library, p161
25 VCH *Warwickshire*, p74,75
26 Ibid. p75
27 ODNB Vol 34 pp351-353

Chapter Two

1   ODNB Vol 19 pp939-940
2   Motkin, Chapter 4
3   Rodwell, op. cit.
4   Motkin, Chapter 4
5   ODNB Vol 38 p48
6   Ibid.
7   Rodwell, op.cit.
8   ODNB Vol 25 pp 284-285
9   Jessica Gorst-Williams, *Elizabeth, The Winter Queen*, p10
10 Moore, p35
11 ODNB Vol 10 pp532-535
12 Antonia Fraser, *Faith and Treason*, p116
13 See online articles about ITV's *The Gunpowder Plot, Exploding the Legend*, 2005.
14 Motkin, Chapter 4
15 Gorst-Williams, p14
16 Ibid. p12
17 Tyack, p58
18 ODNB Vol 25 pp288-289 and Vol 48 pp320-322
19 Ronald G. Asch *Princess Elizabeth Stuart* in ODNB Vol 18 pp85-91
20 ODNB Vol 25 p289
21 ODNB Vol 48 pp320-322

Chapter Three

1   ODNB Vol 14 p 61-62
2   Malcolm R. Smuts, *William Craven, Earl of Craven* ODNB p64
3   Ibid.
4   Ibid. p65
5   Gorst-Williams, p178
6   Ibid. p173
7   Ibid. p163
8   Tyack, Bradley and Pevsner, *The Buildings of England: Berkshire*, pp141,142
9   See article by Nicola Cornick at www.discoverbritainmag.com/ashdown
10 *The Buildings of England: Berkshire*, p321

11 Catalogue in the Coventry City Archives, Herbert Art Gallery and Museum
12 Moore, pp 49,50
13 Henry Benjamin Wheatley, *London Past and Present*, p472
14 Noel Chanan, *William, Earl of Craven and the art of* photography, p178
15 Smuts, pp66,67
16 Tyack, p59
17 Ibid.
18 Smuts, p67

Chapter Four

1   Moore, p54
2   Penelope Stokes, *Craven Country*, etc, p26
3   Ibid. p29
4   ODNB Vol 27 p853
5   Stokes, p27
6   W.H.D. Rouse, *A History of Rugby School*, pp95,98,99
7   See 'The Craven Estate, 1733-1825' at www.corringham.eu/
8   British History Online: *Survey of London*, Vol 18 Chapter 4
9   Chanan, p 22
10 ODNB Vol 8 pp 86-89
11 Moore, pp 62,63
12 Tyack, p62 and Moore, pp64,65
13 ODNB Vol 18, p94
14 Ibid.
15 Chanan, p23
16 *The Memoirs of Harriette Wilson*, Vol I, online
17 Moore, pp69-71 and Tyack, p62
18 Chanan, p33
19 *Annual Register*, 1826, p269
20 Moore, pp73,74
21 Chanan, p35

Chapter Five

1   Chanan, p30
2   Ibid. p14

3   Ibid. p32

4   Ibid. pp38-41

5   Ibid. p117

6   Moore, pp74,75

7   Chanan, p132 and Motkin Chapter 5

8   Chanan, p115

9   Ibid. pp77-82 and additional information kindly provided to the author by Noel Chanan, April, 2018

10   Ibid. p91

11   Ibid. pp165-190

12   Ibid. p194,197

13   Tyack, p63

14   Ibid.

15   Moore, pp79,80

16   Chanan, p203

17   Ibid. p204

18   Stokes, p59

19   Moore, pp81,82

20   See 'Wikipedia' entries for 'House of Carreras' and 'Craven A cigarettes'

Chapter Six

1   *Cornelia (Sherman) Martin, 1843-1920*, Wikitree online

2   Moore, p84

3   Chrystia Freeland, *Plutocrats*, pp6,7

4   Moore, pp 85,86

5   Bonhams sale catalogue *Collectors' Motor Cars and Automobiles at Goodwood*, 29 June 2012

6   Stokes, p62

Chapter Seven

1   Moore, p89

2   Ibid. p91

3   Ibid.

4   Tyack, p63

5   Moore, p94

6   Moore, pp 94-97
7   Motkin, in his Preface
8   Ibid.
9   Motkin, Chapter VII
10 Ibid.
11 Ibid.
12 Moore, p ix
13 *Rugby Advertiser*, 4.7.1991
14 *Coventry Evening Telegraph*, (*CET*) 6.7.1993
15 *CET*, 14.7.1973
16 *CET*, 27.7.1993
17 *CET*, 21.7.1994
18 *CET*, 7.1.1995
19 *CET*, 16.10.1995
20 *CET*, 10.12.1996
21 *Rugby Observer*, 9.10.2017
22 *Coventry Observer*, 24.10.2017

Appendix

1   See *Earl, Playboy, Bad Boy*, online blog by 'The Esoteric Curiosa', posted December 2012.
2   See *History's Headlines by 69 News* online for March 2014.
3   Stokes, p64
4   Ibid.
5   Ibid. p71
6   Ibid. p73
7   See UPI Archives online under 'The curse of the Cravens'.
8   Stokes, p73
9   *Eastbourne Gazette*, 5 September 1990.
10 Stokes, p73
11 *Daily Telegraph* deaths announcement, 28 June 2011.
12 See Sotheby's sale catalogue, *Ashdown House: The Winter Queen and the Earl of Craven*: 27 October 2010.
13 Ibid.
14 Nicola Cornick, *House of Shadows*, Harlequin, 2015, pp392-3.
15 *Newbury Today*, 27.10.2014.

INDEX

Illustrations are marked in bold print.

Index

Index